Discovering Your Personality Type

PERSONALITY TYPES
Using the Enneagram for Self-Discovery

UNDERSTANDING THE ENNEAGRAM
The Practical Guide to Personality Types

DISCOVERING YOUR PERSONALITY TYPE
The Enneagram Questionnaire

ENNEAGRAM TRANSFORMATIONS
Releases and Affirmations for Healing Your Personality Type

DISCOVERING YOUR PERSONALITY TYPE
The New Enneagram Questionnaire

Discovering Your Personality Type

The New Enneagram Questionnaire

Don Richard Riso

Houghton Mifflin Company
Boston · New York

For information about bulk purchases, please see the last page of this book.

Library of Congress Cataloging-in-Publication Data
Riso, Don Richard.
   Discovering your personality type : the new enneagram questionnaire / Don Richard Riso.
      p.   cm.
   ISBN 0-395-71092-8
   1. Riso Enneagram Type Indicator. 2. Enneagram.   I. Title.
BF698.8.R45R57   1995   94-23354
155.2'6 — dc20   CIP

Printed in the United States of America

Line drawings by Mark Desveaux

Printed on recycled paper

QUM 12 11 10

Contents

For Chalfont

Acknowledgments

WHEN I BEGAN writing about the Enneagram, one of my hopes was that publishing books about this wonderful subject would bring me into contact with wonderful people. That hope has come true, and I have been blessed with a life's work that not only seems to me to be worth doing, but with extraordinary people with whom to do it.

I have, first of all, to thank those who have come to my Enneagram Workshops and Enneagram Professional Training Programs for their support and enthusiasm. They are spreading word of the Enneagram, quite literally, around the world. I also want to thank those who have encouraged me to develop a questionnaire. It was not something I was particularly interested in doing until I began to appreciate the usefulness of such an instrument. Readers and students alike can perhaps take satisfaction in knowing that they have had an important role in bringing this project about.

Ruth Hapgood, former senior editor at Houghton Mifflin, was a wise and steady presence during the years in which we worked together, including the period that saw the first edition of this book into print. I am indebted to her for her unflagging support of my work. Thanks also to her able assistant, Sue Ralli, for seeing to the thousand details that were involved in producing the first edition. The excellence of her work was greatly appreciated. I am grateful to Barbara Flanagan and Dorothy Henderson, my manuscript editors, for their sensitive and insightful suggestions. To Steve Lewers, vice president of Houghton Mifflin, go thanks for his interest in the Enneagram and in my efforts.

Since Ruth's retirement, I have been fortunate to work with my new editor, Betsy Lerner, and her assistant, Robert Grover.

Both have been a pleasure to work with, and I look forward to a long, creative association with them.

I am indebted to Phyllis and Gary Cloninger, owners of Enneagram Designs, for their enthusiastic response to my work. Their beautiful products are a superb way to introduce the Enneagram to friends and strangers alike. Best of all, making these products available to the public was the occasion for becoming friends with these wonderful people.

In a similar vein, I would like to acknowledge Rose Mary, Ryan, Regan, Patrick, and Brett O'Boyle, Ruben St. Germain, Charles Aalto, Geoff Edholm, Rick Horton, and Anthony Cassis for their love and support.

Special thanks go to two of my students who are clinical psychologists, Quentin Dinardo, Ph.D., and Betsey Bittlingmaier, Ph.D., for their critique of the first version of this questionnaire. Arlen Baden and Claes Lilja were similarly helpful with comments, critique, and many useful suggestions. Two other students, William Culp, Ph.D., and David Beswick made valuable recommendations concerning the instructions for the RETI which we are continuing to employ in this revised version. I am grateful to everyone who has helped improve the test, including the many students in our Workshops and Trainings who so willingly served as "guinea pigs" during the years of its original conception and continued revision.

A profound and very special acknowledgment goes again to Russ Hudson. I have added his name to the title of this new version both to thank him for his substantive creative input in the first edition of this test, and to credit him publicly for his enormous contributions to this new version.

Since Russ's influence on the development of this field will likely make itself felt for some years to come, a few words about his induction into the world of the Enneagram is probably in order. After reading *Personality Types* in 1988, Russ sought me out for personal consulting, and a friendship soon developed. Russ occasionally visited my office to talk about the Enneagram, spirituality, the Gurdjieff Work, Buddhism, and other topics of mutual interest. During the course of our talks, I showed him early drafts of what was to become the RETI, and his clear and penetrating insights into the types made me realize that he had an unusual talent for this work.

Little did I realize how true that was: I hired Russ in the spring of 1991 as my assistant, and he has quickly established himself as an outstanding Enneagram authority in his own right. He has been responsible for helping me to polish my work and contributed much to my last book, *Enneagram Transformations*. During the development of both versions of this test, he insisted many times that we work harder to improve the questions when I would have gladly given up; he has been the source of scores of new insights into the structure of the Enneagram and the personality types; he has also fertilized our work with insights from other traditions that he has studied and lived for many years.

Since joining Enneagram Personality Types, Inc., Russ has co-taught our Professional Training Programs with me, bringing enormous insight, compassion, and deep spiritual qualities to these events. His contributions have become so numerous and pervasive that I was pleased to name Russ the Executive Director of EPT, and to ask him to become the coauthor of our forthcoming book, *Working with the Enneagram: Transforming the Personality Types*. I personally feel blessed to work with Russ, and I believe that the Enneagram is a much richer field for his presence.

Heartfelt acknowledgment also goes to my mother, Beverly Moreno Pumilia, and my father, Leo Riso, for all that they have given to me. The older I become, the more I realize how my best qualities are really theirs. Finally, my personal adviser, Brian Lawrence Taylor, is invaluable in more ways than I can say. His commitment to my work has been deep and abiding, and without his constant support and guidance, doing it would have been impossible.

Preface

I USED TO think that it was difficult for us to see ourselves clearly because we are too close to ourselves. Now I see that it is difficult because we are too far away, too trapped in illusions and dreams, to know who we really are.

Whether we are too close or too far, whether our fantasies are centered in the past or in the future, the result is the same: we cannot see ourselves because we do not live in the present. We cannot perceive, much less deal with, the realities of our life here and now because our attention is automatically drawn into past and future fantasies by the mechanisms of our personality.

Understanding our personality enables us to break out of the repetitious patterns of our past. However, it is extremely difficult to break out of our old patterns because we are almost totally unaware of them. *The mechanisms of our personality are invisible to us.* We therefore need to find a way to awaken to our true condition, and having awakened, to remain mindful of the siren calls of personality, ever ready to pull us back into old habits and away from the potential that opens up when we live in the present moment.

It is the nature of personality to obscure many dark truths about ourselves. Personality often hides more than it reveals, and discovering one's type is actually not a great accomplishment in and of itself. The real achievement lies in pressing on to learn to distinguish between our inner self (essence) and our personality. To do so, we must cultivate a spiritual practice that allows us to observe ourselves in the midst of our daily lives.

As useful as discovering our type is, it is a much more significant achievement to observe it in action. Indeed, discovering

our personality type presents us with the great challenge of coura-
geously observing ourselves as we really are, no matter what
we find. Without the willingness to see the maneuvers of our personality from moment to moment, transformation cannot take
place. Unless we learn to observe ourselves, finding our type
(with the Enneagram or any other system) will give us little more
than another label with which we can hide from ourselves. If we
only find our type but go no further, ironically, the Enneagram
itself can become an obstacle to our growth.

It is in the act of seeing ourselves objectively, however, that
something lets go in us: suddenly we find ourselves in a state of
increased freedom and clarity in which we discover that at our
deepest *we are not our personality*. When we experience this
truth, transformation becomes possible. Without trying to do
anything to "fix" ourselves, the act of bringing awareness to the
moment causes our essential self to arise and our personality to
lose its grip over us. As we become increasingly liberated from
our personality, our essence reveals its many facets — acceptance, love, authenticity, forgiveness, compassion, courage, joy,
strength, and presence — as well as many other manifestations
of the human spirit. By moving beyond merely knowing our type
to the ability to see ourselves as we are, the shift from personality
to essence takes place and we discover that we can live differently. We discover that we can be free.

REAL SELF-KNOWLEDGE is thus an extraordinarily valuable
commodity, and an Enneagram questionnaire — indeed, any
questionnaire that aims to help us discover our personality type
— cannot provide it by itself. At best, all a test can do is point
out what type you are. While the first version of the *Riso Enneagram Type Indicator* was a useful instrument that enabled people
to discover their type, it had a number of limitations.

Some are inherent in the nature of any question-and-answer
test. No test can be foolproof or one hundred percent accurate.
After several years of experience with test construction, I have
come to the conclusion that it is virtually impossible to devise a
questionnaire which is much over ninety percent accurate, and

any claims to having done so should be met with skepticism. With this version of the RHETI, however, I believe we are in the ninety percent range of accuracy, but beyond that it may well be impossible to go, for some of the following reasons.

One of the primary limitations of the first version of the RETI (again, as with any personality test) can be traced to an essential contradiction in tests that rely on self-reporting: it takes some degree of self-knowledge to take a type test, yet this is often the very thing that is in short supply.

Because many people lack self-knowledge, they are at a loss about what is true when a questionnaire asks them to report on their attitudes or behaviors. At the heart of the problem is the fact that each of us has a certain self-image that does not include everything about us. For example, we may be far more aggressive than we realize, or, we may not be as sensitive, loving, dependable, or outgoing as our self-image has led us to believe. One of the values of the Enneagram is to help us correct our distorted notions about ourselves — but until we can acknowledge our "blind spots" we will not be able to recognize them either in ourselves or in a test.

It is also in the very nature of certain personality types to have difficulty identifying themselves. The three primary types (see *Personality Types*, 308–310) — Threes, Sixes, and Nines — probably have the most trouble because their identity is rooted in their identifications with others. They live through others, or else, live through the real or imagined reactions of others to them. Either way, they do not see themselves directly; testing these types is therefore extremely difficult. Of course, all of the types present other problems caused by self-deception, self-justification, and the desire to "look good."

The first version of the RETI was also subject to the sorts of problems encountered in other self-scored tests: people often skipped questions or entire pages, or made mistakes in arithmetic as they added their scores. Some did not understand the vocabulary, did not follow the instructions, or got impatient and answered the questions arbitrarily. Other errors were more subtle: while some respondents did not have the self-knowledge to answer the questions appropriately, others knew the Enneagram types only too well, and were able to skew the answers to make the test confirm the type they wanted to be. Others read the statements in unusual ways, bringing to them interpretations and associations that completely changed the intended meaning of the questions. Others overanalyzed the questions and became confused by hairsplitting and thinking of fantastic situations in which both of the statements might possibly be true of them. When one considers all of the potential sources of error that can be introduced in test-taking, it is a wonder that any personality test ever comes out at all.

Despite these problems, in retrospect, the first version of the RETI seems to have been about seventy-five to eighty percent accurate for determining basic personality type. While carefully reading Enneagram books and going to workshops is the most commonly used way to identify or confirm one's type, a substantial number of people will still be helped by having an accurate personality type indicator available. (It is also important to recognize that significant differences exist between the various Enneagram authors and teachers; their descriptions of the personality types vary, and people can easily become confused by the contradictory interpretations. Thus, going to workshops and reading books will not infallibly reveal anyone's type.)

Insights obtained from a test, workshop, or an Enneagram teacher should be used only as corroborative pieces of evidence in the process of self-discovery. It is unwise to expect any single method to be the only way to discover our type. The responsibility for finding out who we are always lies with us. Insights from any method should be considered along with all the other available evidence before we come to any final conclusions. Talking to friends, reading the descriptions in *Personality Types, Understanding the Enneagram*, and in this book, reflecting on the Releases and Affirmations in *Enneagram Transformations*, attending workshops, and above all, relying on your own introspection over a period of time are the best ways to discover your type with confidence.

Even so, the intention behind developing the RHETI was not

merely to give people a shortcut for determining their personality type. If the Enneagram is to continue to gain mainstream and academic acceptance, the empirical validation of this system is necessary, and having a reliable questionnaire is essential. That process began with the first version of this test, which, despite its limitations, has become the recognized standard in the field, and will be accelerated with the publication of this more accurate version.*

Differences between the original RETI and Version 2.0

Naturally, we hope that this new version of the RHETI will be more accurate, more useful in self-help and therapeutic situations, more evocative, and easier to take. Toward these ends, many changes in the test have been made.

All of the statements in Version 2.0 of the RHETI have been put in the *past* tense to remind people to take the test from that point of view. Since people were instructed to take the RETI "as they have been most of their lives," it seemed helpful to have the statements reflect this past-orientation. (After you have taken the RHETI from the point of view of the past, you may also wish to take it "as you are now," in the present; when you do so, you must, of course, remind yourself to answer the past-tense questions as if they referred to the present.) The statements have also been rearranged and the order of the columns changed to make this new version easier to take.

Furthermore, approximately eighty-five percent of the original questions have been replaced by new questions in this revised version. After extensive testing and analysis, we replaced many

---

* The editors of Time-Life Books have chosen my work as the clearest and most useful interpretation of the Enneagram available. They have excerpted the descriptions of the personality types and featured some of the questions from the first version of the RETI in *The Enigma of Personality,* a volume in their psychology series "Journey Through the Mind and Body." It may be obtained by calling 1-800-621-7026.

questions which were not working well enough, as well as those which proved not to be working well at all. Sometimes, we were forced to replace an otherwise workable question because it became clear that too many people were reading meanings into it that were not intended. In other instances, we replaced a statement because it turned out to be too ambiguous.

Insights we received from those attending our Workshops and Trainings revealed new dimensions of the types that we had not previously known. The types are extremely subtle and complex, and we are constantly uncovering new aspects of them. Over time, we also learned how best to work with the "forced choice" format itself, drafting pairs of statements in which people could better discern which of the two statements was more true of them.

Given the multiple parameters in which we had to operate, the conceptual problems mounted quickly: the statements must specify something people can recognize in themselves while avoiding issues that are too abstract or so subtle that only a person in analysis would be aware of them; the statements must not describe attitudes that are either too healthy or too unhealthy, particularly the latter, since experience indicated that people did not respond honestly to anything that would reflect too negatively on them; there must be no sex bias to the statements; ideally, the statements should not simply negate each other ("I like ice cream" versus "I don't like ice cream"); preferably, the statements should avoid "Enneagram jargon" and other language that would alert readers to which type was being tested; the statements must all discriminate to a level of seventy percent or better between the two types being tested, and the seven remaining types must split relatively evenly with four types agreeing with one statement and three agreeing with the other; both statements must reflect attitudes or behavior at the same Level of Development for their respective types so that one statement did not seem to be healthier and therefore more attractive than the alternative.

Several other parameters also had to be kept in mind as we

drafted statements for the test. Needless to say, this has been a time-consuming and arduous task, but we feel that this new version is a significant advance that will help the entire field progress.

New Instructions & Suggestions

You can take the RHETI several different ways, although we have found that the most accurate approach is to take the test from the point of view of the past, "as you have been most of your life." (This does not mean to take it as you were in childhood, but rather, as you were as a young adult.)

This is especially true if you have been in psychological or spiritual work and feel that you have changed óver time. If you have changed significantly, it is important to identify what you were like *before* the changes in your personality took place. (What we believe you will find is that your basic type has remained the same, while the overall pattern of your scores may have shifted significantly.)

If you would like to take the RHETI several times, take it first as you were in the past, then, answering in a different color of ink or pencil, take the test again *as you are in the present.* As just noted, the RHETI should indicate that your basic type is the same, although the profile produced by the balance of the other Functions (see pages 80–83) will be somewhat different.

Discovering your dominant wing (or auxiliary type) is possible with the RHETI, although this will be less reliable than other results of the test, especially for the primary types, Three, Six, and Nine. (See pages 14–15 and 84–85 of this book for a discussion.) Remember that the purpose of the RHETI is to help people discover their basic personality type; any other information above and beyond that is an extra dividend.

While we believe that it is best to answer all 144 pairs of statements, you may also wish to skip those few questions that you honestly feel do not pertain to you in any way. Please be careful, however, not to skip over those statements that you merely find

difficult to answer. It is useful to wrestle with difficult statements, but you can skip those few that you feel are totally irrele-
vant to you.

As we have already suggested (*Discovering Your Personality
Type*, 26–27), you can take the RHETI with someone who knows
you well, such as a spouse, close friend, or therapist. Doing so
may yield more accurate results because others often can see you
more clearly than you can see yourself. Further, you can have
your spouse, close friend, or therapist take the test for you, as if
they were you. This method will also yield valuable results and
likely be the occasion for a stimulating conversation.

After you have finished taking the RHETI one or more different
ways, you can go to Section 7 of this book, "The Statements
Arranged by Type," and take the RHETI as a "weighted choice"
test. You may change the format of the test by assigning a numerical ranking to each of the statements, first for the two or three
types in which you scored highest, and if you have time, for the
remaining six or seven types.

In the margin of the book, or on a piece of paper, rank the
statements from 1 to 5, according to how much you agree that
they reflect your past attitudes and behavior, with 1 meaning
"never or almost never," and 5 meaning "always, or almost always," then add your scores for each type. Note that there are 32
statements for each personality type; your lowest potential score
for any type would therefore be 32 if you gave a score of 1 for
each statement. Your highest potential score would be 160 if you
scored 5 for each of the 32 statements. The type which has the
highest numerical score should indicate your basic personality
type. As noted above, the RHETI in its original "forced choice"
format does not always discriminate for the correct wing, especially for types Three, Six, and Nine. The "weighted choice" format may do so more accurately.

You can extract more information from the RHETI by adding
your scores in several other significant groups: first, according to
Triad, which indicates whether your assets and liabilities occur
in your *thinking center* (the Doing Triad — types Five, Six, and
Seven), *feeling center* (the Feeling Triad — types Two, Three, and

Four), or *instinctual center* (the Relating Triad — types Eight, Nine, and One).

A second, often more illuminating way to analyze your scores is to add them according to what we call the "Hornevian Groups." In *Personality Types,* I was the first Enneagram author to note that the psychiatrist Karen Horney's aggressive types, or those who "move against people" correspond to the Enneagram types Three, Seven, and Eight. Her compliant types, or those who "move toward people," correspond to the Enneagram types One, Two, and Six, and her withdrawn types, or those who "move away from people," correspond to types Four, Five, and Nine.

Add your scores for the withdrawn types (Four, Five, and Nine), your scores for the compliant types (One, Two, and Six), and your scores for the aggressive types (Three, Seven, and Eight) to see the Group in which you are highest.

This may help you to analyze scores in ambiguous cases, such as the example of a man who was clearly an Eight (according to an experienced Enneagram teacher) but who tested highest as a One, with Eight coming in a very close second. However, by adding the scores of his three aggressive types (Three, Seven, and Eight) it was clear that he was one of the aggressive types. Moreover, the Seven was his third highest score, which is consistent with his being an Eight with a Seven-wing. Once he heard the description of the Eight during the workshop, he agreed that that was his type, and the correct diagnosis was possible. In another case, a person who had mistyped himself as a Five had very high scores in the aggressive types, and further interviewing and introspection indicated that the person was in fact a Three and not a Five. His low scores in the withdrawn group also indirectly confirmed this analysis.

Please note a special *caveat.* If you are a woman thirty years or older, and especially if you are from a background in which women were taught to fulfill the role of the caretaker, it is best to question any high Two scores you may get with the RHETI. Try as we might, we have found it difficult in the forced choice format to eliminate the tendency of women to come out falsely as Twos. While we believe that Version 2.0 has fewer instances of false Two scores, it is not foolproof in this regard. Therefore, if you are a woman and have come out with Two as your highest score, look at the next highest score to see if that type describes you better. For example, a woman at a workshop tested as a Two (24) and next as a Six (23). After hearing the description of the Six, she realized that it fit her completely and that she was not a Two. Another woman tested as a Two (28) and a Nine (26); she turned out to be a Nine who was taught to play the role of the nurturing mother, a role she completely fulfilled. In a sense, she is a Nine playing the role of a Two, as her life history and personal sharing indicated.

For certain other types, we have seen that the person's actual type is sometimes indicated by one of the top two to three scores instead of the highest score. Besides Twos, other types present serious problems to anyone designing an Enneagram test. Nines, for example, tend to see themselves in almost all of the types, particularly the types of those persons with whom they have identified. They typically have relatively "flat" or evenly distributed scores for all nine types, with Nine among the top two or three scores. Sixes typically overanalyze the test, and have problems deciding which type they are because they cannot make a decision about which of the alternative statements is more true of them. Sevens typically misread the statements, or take the test so quickly that they make other mistakes. For these and other reasons, we have commonly seen Nines misidentified as Twos, Fours, and Fives, Sixes coming out as a wide variety of different types, and Sevens testing as Twos and Fours. Threes often mistype themselves as Ones, Fours, or Fives, and Twos as Fours.

On the other hand, the RHETI is sometimes more correct than our preconceptions and expectations. For example, a person who thinks he or she is a Four may well test as a Six because the person really is a Six. People who are either new to the Enneagram or who have been confused by different interpretations often misidentify themselves, and when the RHETI produces a result other than the one they expect, they usually think that the RHETI is wrong.

Unfortunately, the only way to resolve the problem of which

diagnosis is correct is for the person to keep an open mind, to go over the RHETI with someone who knows him or her well, and to carefully read the descriptions of the types in question. In time, the accurate type will become clear.

Naturally, even this new version of the RHETI is not perfect. Like all the work being done on the Enneagram, it is a work in progress. While based on an ancient symbol, the application of the Enneagram to psychology is modern, and our understanding of it as a model for human nature is constantly deepening and evolving. Just as there is no ancient "oral tradition" source for the teachings and materials from which Enneagram authors can draw material, so too there is no definitive source to which we can turn for insight. The usefulness and brilliance of the Enneagram lies simply in the fact that it "cleaves the diamond of the psyche along its proper internal lines" (*DYPT*, 6). It is an extraordinary map that illuminates our way as we discover more about a mysterious reality: human nature — ever the same, ever new.

Don Richard Riso

New York City
March 1994

PART·ONE

PLEASE NOTE!
If you would like to take the *Riso-Hudson Enneagram Type Indicator* right away, go to page 25 in this book now. It is not necessary to know anything about the Enneagram (pronounced "ANY-a-gram") to obtain valid results from this questionnaire.

1. A Brief Introduction to the Enneagram

Understanding Ourselves and Others

The Enneagram is extraordinarily useful *because it works.* It is the clearest, most accurate method available for understanding ourselves and those who are important to us. It helps us understand why we do not easily get along with certain people while with others we instantly feel that we are old friends. Understanding the Enneagram is like having a pair of special glasses that allows us to see beneath the surface of people with amazing clarity: we may in fact see them more clearly than they see themselves.

The insights the Enneagram gives us can change our lives, and those who have gotten to know it cannot imagine how they once got along without it. It is as if they had been born color-blind and were suddenly able to see the world in all its subtle hues for the first time. They are thrilled to uncover what had been "right in front of their noses" but was obscure and hidden from view. The Enneagram opens up whole new vistas for us, new depths of comprehension, new levels of meaning. Knowledge such as this is not obtained without paying a price; however, there can be no going back to our former blindness once we understand the Enneagram. The world, others, and we will be different forever.

Moreover, there are as many uses for the Enneagram as there are individuals who use it. Those who are in therapy or in one of the Twelve Step Programs or other kinds of psychospiritual work will find it an invaluable source of insight into their childhood and why they have become the people they are. Those in intimate relationships will benefit from understanding more about themselves and their partners since relationships depend, among other things, on honesty and trust. No relationship can work unless both parties bring sensitivity and insight to it, particularly when conflicts and misunderstandings arise. Understanding what others need, want, and fear, how they express themselves — as well as what they are afraid of expressing — is the best way to keep a relationship alive and growing. And understanding what we need, want, fear, and are afraid of expressing is the best way to keep our own psyches healthy.

Having insight into human behavior is also an enormously valuable skill. The Enneagram has begun to attract the attention of businesses and corporations looking for ways to increase their employees' productivity and, ultimately, their profitability. While the Enneagram is primarily a profound psychological and spiritual tool, it is also highly practical because its insights are so on target that they save a great deal of time and frustration for management and employees alike. The Enneagram can be used for hiring the "right" person for a particular job, for teaching executives to manage more effectively, for customer service, for clarifying a corporate image — a corporate "personality type," so to speak — or for building a more profitable sales force. Team building, marketing, corporate communication, and conflict resolution — among its many applications — are more effective when insights from the Enneagram are applied in the business world.

Naturally, however, if the Enneagram is to be used for self-understanding, for relationships, for therapy, or for business, one's personality type (and those of others) must be accurately assessed. This questionnaire, the *Riso-Hudson Enneagram Type Indicator*, provides a reliable tool for that purpose. Those who are already acquainted with the Enneagram have intuitively sensed that this system works; the RHETI attempts to complement intuition by verifying the personality types empirically. If the Enneagram is to become more widely known, its intuitive validity will have to be corroborated by hard evidence. This questionnaire is offered as a step toward the scientific validation of the Enneagram.

We must remember that while the Enneagram has many practical uses, its primary function is to help us understand who we are so that we can be transformed by transcending our personality. In a sense, the Enneagram works by negating itself: the more clearly we see ourselves, the more we begin to move beyond personality, and the less we need the Enneagram. Unless we have already learned to move beyond ourselves, however, most of us still need the wisdom this system has to offer.

THE ENNEAGRAM was brought to the West by the Russian spiritual teacher George Ivanovitch Gurdjieff around the turn of the century and further developed by the Bolivian mystic Oscar Ichazo beginning in the 1960s. The psychiatrist Claudio Naranjó, who had studied with Ichazo, brought the Enneagram to the United States in 1970, and, within a few years, awareness of this powerful typology quickly spread around North America. In 1975, I began developing the Enneagram in the light of modern psychology, adding my own insights and discoveries to the original body of knowledge. You can find more about the history and development of the Enneagram in Section 8.*

The early traditions begun by Gurdjieff and Ichazo were the first attempts to communicate the Enneagram to a modern audience; my efforts have been mainly to develop the descriptions of the personality types (and the underlying theory) so that the Enneagram could become accessible to a wider audience.

We are primarily concerned with the psychospiritual uses of this system: we discover our likeness in the mirror of the Enneagram, thereby gaining extraordinary insight into ourselves. What is particularly intriguing is that this system corroborates many of the findings of the *Diagnostic and Statistical Manual of Mental*

---

* For more information about the history and transmission of the Enneagram and about Gurdjieff, Ichazo, and my further development of this system, see my *Personality Types* (1987) and *Understanding the Enneagram* (1990). Parenthetical references to those books are abbreviated as *PT* and *UTE* and include page numbers from them. Since these books contain full bibliographies about the Enneagram and related topics, that information has not been repeated here.

Disorders, third edition (revised), of the American Psychiatric Association, the *DSM*-III(R).

In *Understanding the Enneagram*, we saw that the Enneagram improves on the typologies proposed by modern psychology by its specificity, comprehensiveness, and elegance (209–29). It organizes observations about human nature by consolidating what has already been discovered as well as by suggesting new avenues for investigation. By "cleaving the diamond" of the psyche along its proper internal lines, the Enneagram presents us with the categories that we actually find in everyday life.

One of the primary things to understand about the Enneagram is that we find ourselves reflected in the whole of it. From one point of view, the personality types are metaphors for the various psychological functions operating in each of us. (See Section 6 for more on the Functions.) We develop into one of the nine personality types because our consciousness has been formed in a certain way as a result of our childhood experiences and heredity. Our basic personality type is, in a sense, as much a defense against our environment as an adaptive reaction to it. The remaining eight personality types (which we develop to greater or lesser degrees throughout our lives) represent the other potentials of our psyche and are also important parts of who we are.

It is also worth realizing that this typology is not the sole province of academics — much less of the mystics, priests, or psychologists who originally developed it. The Enneagram belongs to everyone because it is accessible and helps people from all walks of life make sense of themselves and their relationships. With its precision, practicality, and universality, the Enneagram can reinvigorate many aspects of psychology and spirituality.

People all over the world are responding to the Enneagram because they see their experience reflected in it. They are embracing it as one of the most important discoveries of their lives, something that has helped them make sense of what previously seemed impenetrably ambiguous or, worse, utterly chaotic. Once people grasp the essentials of this extraordinary system, they can participate in the endless adventure of deepening their understanding of themselves and their fellow humans. Who knows what benefits will accrue as new generations are able to draw on the insights of the Enneagram throughout their lives?

IN THE LAST analysis, the Enneagram is extraordinarily valuable because it makes traveling the path of self-knowledge more sure. By helping us see our behaviors and motivations, desires and fears, attitudes and defenses, the Enneagram brings to light what was formerly hidden from us. It also provides a way out of our conflicts and confusions and helps us to be hopeful in moments of darkness and despair. It demonstrates that we are not alone in our struggles because, in so many unexpected ways, we are like everyone else.

The Enneagram is thus a *microcosm* of each of us because it provides us with a map of our own consciousness. It is also a *macrocosm* that displays the fundamental number of personality types that are necessary and sufficient for the human economy. (Too few and we would be virtually identical, which we clearly are not; too many and human beings would be incomprehensible mysteries to each other. The human family would be no more than distant cousins who have little understanding of, much less compassion for, each other.)

Furthermore, the Enneagram is of immense importance because without self-knowledge, freeing ourselves from conflicts and neuroses would be virtually impossible. Once we have been drawn into neuroses, we find it increasingly difficult to choose what is best for us, so it becomes even more difficult to work our way out of our problems. We can reverse the vicious circle created by becoming trapped in our typical fixations by fully acknowledging and releasing our fears and habitual tendencies. If we do so, we find that life becomes easier because our time and energy can be used for living creatively rather than be wasted in internal turmoil and conflicts. We also discover that, once we have begun to recognize our automatic responses, we can let go of them, thus transcending our old states. We then naturally find ourselves drawn to healthy ways of living and relating.

Moreover, having an accurate map of our psychic landscape is a supremely practical thing because most of us have not acquired the habit of introspection, nor do we belong to an authentic spiritual school that could guide us along our path. Our materialistic Western culture does not encourage taking time from daily routines to meditate or practice spiritual disciplines so that we can acquire the resources necessary for our inner journey.

Of these resources, freedom from inner conflicts, delusions, and fears is among the most important. Before we can go forward we need to go inward to discover a part of ourselves that is not conflicted, deluded, or fearful. By understanding the mechanical aspects of our personality (that is, our automatic, reactive, defensive patterns), we learn how to avoid them in the future. By learning nonidentification with our personality, we become free from the shackles of our personality. Therefore, the paradox of the Enneagram is this: *We study the Enneagram because it is necessary to understand how our personality operates before we can become free of it.*

In the end, the Enneagram can be thought of as a treasure map that indicates where the secret riches of the innermost self can be discovered. Pointing out each type's path of self-transcendence is thus the Enneagram's most profound gift. But the Enneagram is only a map, and it is up to us to make the journey: only we can accept the daily challenge and adventure that is our life. The Enneagram takes us to the threshold of spirit and freedom, transcendence and liberation, self-surrender and self-actualization. Once we have arrived at that uncharted land, we can begin to recognize our truest self, the self beyond personality, the self of essence. That self, of course, cannot be tested by a questionnaire, but only by life itself.

How the Enneagram Works

The object of this questionnaire is to identify your basic personality type; if you answer the statements in the *Riso-Hudson Enneagram Type Indicator* honestly, it will do so with a high degree of reliability.

Since this book is also a brief introduction to the Enneagram, the following explanation will be helpful for beginners. As you will see, only a few simple concepts are needed to understand how the Enneagram works. This system, however, is ultimately subtle and complex, as you will appreciate the more you use it in your life. For more guidelines, consult *Personality Types* (23–46), from which this presentation has been condensed and revised, and for further clarification see *Understanding the Enneagram* (24–34).

Structure

The Enneagram's structure may look complicated, although it is actually simple. It will help you understand the Enneagram if you sketch it yourself.

Draw a circle and mark nine equidistant points on its circumference. Designate each point by a number from one to nine, with nine at the top, for symmetry and by convention. Each point represents one of the nine basic personality types.

The nine points on the circumference are also connected with each other by the inner lines of the Enneagram. Note that points Three, Six, and Nine form an equilateral triangle. The remaining six points are connected in the following order: One connects with Four, Four with Two, Two with Eight, Eight with Five,

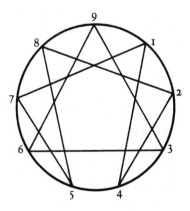

The Enneagram

Five with Seven, and Seven with One. These six points form an irregular hexagram. The meaning of these inner lines will be discussed shortly.

Your Basic Personality Type

From one point of view, the Enneagram can be seen as a set of nine personality types, with each number on the Enneagram denoting one distinct type. It is common to find a little of yourself in all nine types, although one of them should stand out as being closest to yourself. This is your *basic personality type.*

Everyone emerges from childhood as *one* of the nine types, with both genetics and childhood relationships with parents or other significant persons playing an important role in the process. By the time children are four or five years old, their consciousness has developed sufficiently to have a separate sense of self. Although their identity is still very fluid, children at this age begin to establish themselves and find ways of fitting into the world on their own. Which basic personality type individuals eventually become reflects the totality of all childhood factors (including genetics) that influenced their development. (For more about the origins of each personality type, see *UTE*, 36–39.)

Several more points can be made about the basic personality type itself. First, people do not change from one basic type to another. Second, the descriptions of the personality types are universal and apply equally to males and females, since no type is inherently masculine or feminine. Third, not everything in the description of your basic type will apply to you all the time because you fluctuate constantly among the healthy, average, and unhealthy traits that make up your personality type. Fourth, the Enneagram uses numbers to designate each of the types because numbers are value-neutral — they imply the whole range of attitudes and behaviors of each type without specifying anything either positive or negative. Unlike the labels used in psychiatry, numbers provide an unbiased, shorthand way of indicating a lot about a person without being pejorative. Nor is the numerical ranking of the types significant. A larger number is no better than a smaller number; it is not better to be a Nine than a Two because nine is a higher number.

Fifth, no type is inherently better or worse than any other. While all the personality types have unique assets and liabilities, some types are often more desirable than others in any given culture or group. Furthermore, for one reason or another, you may not be happy being a particular type. You may feel that your type is "handicapped" in some way. As you learn more about all the types, you will see that just as each has unique capacities, each has different limitations. If some types are more esteemed in Western society than others, it is because of the qualities that society rewards, not because of any superior value of those types. The ideal is to become *your best self,* not to envy the assets of another type.

Identifying Your Basic Personality Type

If taken properly, the RHETI will identify your basic personality type for you. This short section is included for those who want to understand the Enneagram before taking the questionnaire or for those who want to explain the Enneagram to others.

As you think about your personality, which of the following nine roles fits you best most of the time? Or, to put it differently, if you were to describe yourself in one word, which of the following words would come closest?

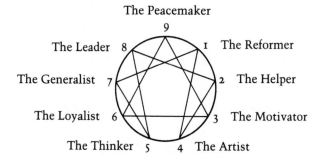

The Riso Enneagram Type Names

These one-word descriptors can be expanded into four-word sets of traits. Keep in mind that these are merely highlights and do not represent the full spectrum of each type.

The *One* is principled, orderly, perfectionistic, and self-righteous.
The *Two* is caring, generous, possessive, and manipulative.
The *Three* is adaptable, ambitious, image-conscious, and hostile.
The *Four* is intuitive, individualistic, self-absorbed, and depressive.
The *Five* is perceptive, original, provocative, and eccentric.
The *Six* is engaging, responsible, defensive, and paranoid.
The *Seven* is enthusiastic, accomplished, excessive, and manic.
The *Eight* is self-confident, decisive, dominating, and combative.
The *Nine* is receptive, optimistic, complacent, and disengaged.

The Triads

The Enneagram is a 3 × 3 arrangement of nine personality types *in three Triads.* There are three types in the *Feeling Triad,* three in the *Doing Triad,* and three in the *Relating Triad,* as shown below. The inclusion of each type in its Triad is not arbitrary. Moreover, each type can be seen as part of a dialectic within each Triad. Each Triad consists of three personality types that have in common the assets and liabilities of that Triad. For example, personality type Four has unique strengths and liabilities involv-

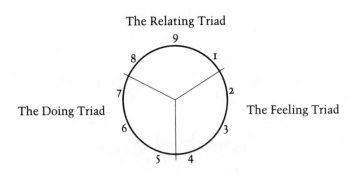

The Triads of the Enneagram

ing its feelings, which is why it is in the Feeling Triad. Likewise, the Eight's assets and liabilities involve its ability to relate to the environment, which is why it is in the Relating Triad, and so forth for all nine personality types.

One of the types overdevelops (or overexpresses) the characteristic faculty of the Triad, another type underdevelops (or underexpresses) the faculty, and the third is most out of touch (or most blocked) with the faculty. These relationships are depicted in the following illustration.

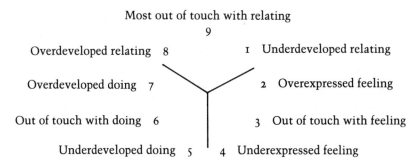

Most out of touch with relating
9

Overdeveloped relating   8   1   Underdeveloped relating

Overdeveloped doing   7   2   Overexpressed feeling

Out of touch with doing   6   3   Out of touch with feeling

Underdeveloped doing   5   4   Underexpressed feeling

The Dialectical Structure of the Triads

We can briefly see what this means by examining each type, Triad by Triad. In the Feeling Triad, *Twos* overexpress their feelings, excessively stating only their positive feelings for others while repressing their negative feelings (such as anger and resentment at not being appreciated enough.) *Threes* are the most out of touch with their feelings. They have learned to put aside their own feelings in order to be more effective in their performance.

Fours underexpress their feelings since they often feel ashamed of themselves, their needs, desires, and impulses; instead of revealing themselves directly, they do so indirectly through some form of art or aesthetic living. (For more brief sketches of the types of the Feeling Triad, see *PT*, 30–31.)

In the Doing Triad, *Fives* substitute thinking for doing, so that their ability to do remains undeveloped. They find it difficult to bring closure to their quest for information and understanding and to act on what they know. Instead, they go around endlessly in ever more complex, abstract thoughts. *Sixes* are the most out of touch with their ability to act on their own without the sanction and guidance of others. Ironically, Sixes also tend to resist and react against the very people they have looked to for security and direction. *Sevens* have overdeveloped their ability to act by doing things all the time. To avoid anxiety, they give in to their impulses until they become hyperactive, escapist, and manic, eventually flying out of control. (For more brief sketches of the types of the Doing Triad, see *PT*, 31–32.)

In the Relating Triad, *Eights* have overdeveloped their ability to relate to the environment because they see themselves as bigger than everyone else. They dominate everything and everyone, controlling their world so that it will conform to the way they want it to be. *Nines* are most out of touch with their ability to relate to the environment since they relate to life through an idealized vision of reality (including an idealization of other people). They are out of touch with their own sense of self because they have merged with others and have subordinated themselves to their identifications. *Ones* have underdeveloped their ability to relate to the environment in the sense that they feel themselves to be less than an ideal that they constantly strive to attain. They also feel that they must control themselves according to the dictates of their conscience, the source of their strictures on themselves and others. (For more brief sketches of the types of the Relating Triad, see *PT*, 33–34. For distinctions between the "primary" personality types and the "secondary" types, see *PT*, 26, 308–10.)

The Wing

No one is a pure personality type: everyone is a unique mixture of his or her basic type and one of the two types adjacent to it on the circumference of the Enneagram. One of the two types next to your basic type is your *wing*.

Your basic type dominates your overall personality, while the wing complements it and adds important, sometimes contradictory, elements to your total personality. Your wing is the "second side" of your personality, and it must be taken into consideration to better understand yourself or someone else. For example, if you are a personality type Nine, you will have *either* a One-wing or an Eight-wing, and your personality as a whole can best be understood by considering the traits of the Nine with those of either the One or the Eight as they uniquely blend in you.

There is disagreement among the various interpretations of the Enneagram about whether individuals have one or two wings. Strictly speaking, everyone has two wings — in the restricted sense that both of the types adjacent to your basic type are operative in your personality since each person possesses the potentials of all nine types. However, this is not what is usually meant by "having two wings," and proponents of the so-called two-wing theory believe that both wings operate more or less equally in everyone's personality. (For example, they believe that every Nine would have roughly equal amounts of his or her Eight and One wings.)

Observation and testing of people leads to the conclusion that people have varying proportions of wings, and that most people have a *dominant* wing. There are a few cases in which individuals seem to have two "balanced" wings; however, it is far more common to find combinations of main type and single dominant wing that result in distinct blends. For example, Twos with Three-wings are noticeably different from Twos with One-wings; in fact, they can be distinguished as separate subtypes. It is therefore clearer to refer simply to a type's "wing" as opposed to its "dominant wing," since the two terms represent the same concept.

It is, of course, necessary to identify your basic type before you can assess which wing you have. Besides indicating your basic type, the *Riso-Hudson Enneagram Type Indicator* may also indicate your wing. Even so, the best way to definitely determine your wing is to read the full descriptions in *Personality Types* of the two types adjacent to your basic type and decide which best applies to you.

Directions of Integration and Disintegration

The nine personality types of the Enneagram are not static categories: they reflect our psychological growth and deterioration. The numbers on the Enneagram are connected in a sequence that denotes the Direction of Integration (health, self-actualization) and the Direction of Disintegration (unhealth, neurosis) for each personality type. In other words, as you become more healthy or unhealthy, you will develop in different ways, as indicated by the lines of the Enneagram *from your basic type.*

The *Direction of Disintegration* for each type is indicated by the sequence of numbers 1-4-2-8-5-7-1. This means that types in their average to unhealthy Levels will exhibit some of the average to unhealthy behaviors of the type in their Direction of Disintegration. For example, an average to unhealthy One will exhibit some of the average to unhealthy behaviors of the Four, an average to unhealthy Two will exhibit some average to unhealthy Eight behaviors, an Eight will exhibit some Five behaviors, a Five will exhibit some Seven behaviors, and an average to unhealthy Seven will behave like an average to unhealthy One. (An easy way to remember the sequence is to realize that 1-4, or 14, doubles to 28, and that doubles to 57 — or almost so. Thus, 1-4-2-8-5-7 — and the sequence returns to 1 and begins again.) Likewise, on the equilateral triangle, the sequence is 9-6-3-9: under stress, an average to unhealthy Nine will sometimes behave like an average to unhealthy Six, an average to unhealthy Six will sometimes behave like a Three, and a Three will sometimes behave like a Nine. (You can remember this sequence if you think of the numerical values diminishing as the types become more unhealthy. For a longer explanation and examples, see *PT*, 38–39.) You can see how this works by following the direction of the arrows on the following Enneagram.

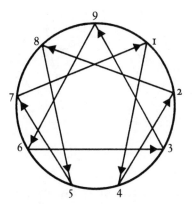

The Direction of Disintegration

1–4–2–8–5–7–1
9–6–3–9

The *Direction of Integration* for each type is indicated by the *reverse* of the sequences for disintegration. Each type moves toward integration in a direction that is the opposite of its unhealthy direction. Thus, the sequence for the Direction of Integration is 1-7-5-8-2-4-1: an integrating One goes to Seven, an integrating Seven goes to Five, an integrating Five goes to Eight, an integrating Eight goes to Two, an integrating Two goes to Four, and an integrating Four goes to One. On the equilateral triangle, the sequence is 9-3-6-9: an integrating Nine will go to Three, an integrating Three will go to Six, and an integrating Six will go to Nine. You can see how this works by following the direction of the arrows on the following Enneagram.

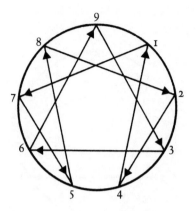

The Direction of Integration

1–7–5–8–2–4–1
9–3–6–9

It is not necessary to have separate Enneagrams for the Direction of Integration and the Direction of Disintegration. Both directions can be shown on one Enneagram by eliminating the arrows and connecting the proper points with plain lines.

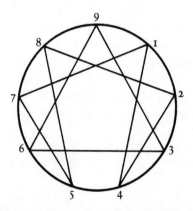

The Direction of Integration

1–7–5–8–2–4–1
9–3–6–9

The Direction of Disintegration

1–4–2–8–5–7–1
9–6–3–9

No matter which personality type you are, the types in *both* your Direction of Integration and your Direction of Disintegration are important influences. To obtain a complete picture of yourself (or of someone else), you must take into consideration the basic type and wing as well as the two types in the Directions of Integration and Disintegration. The factors represented by those *four* types blend into your total personality and provide the framework for understanding the influences operating in you. For example, no one is simply a personality type Two. A Two has either a One-wing or a Three-wing, and the Two's Direction of Disintegration (Eight) and its Direction of Integration (Four) also play important parts in his or her overall personality. (For more details, see *PT*, 39–40.)

Ultimately, the goal is for each of us to "move around" the Enneagram, integrating what each type symbolizes and acquiring the healthy potentials of *all the types*. The ideal is to become a balanced, fully functioning person who can draw on the strengths of each type as needed. Each of the types of the Enneagram symbolizes different important aspects of what we need to achieve this end. (See Section 6 on the Functions.) The personality type we have become is therefore less important than how well (or badly) we use our type as the beginning point of our self-development and self-transcendence.

The Continuum of Traits

There is an internal structure within each personality type. That structure is the Continuum of the nine Levels of Development, which forms the personality type itself.

You have doubtless noticed that you change constantly, sometimes for the better, sometimes for the worse. Understanding the Continuum makes it clear that when you do, you are shifting within the spectrum of motivations, traits, and defenses that make up your personality type.

To understand an individual accurately, it is necessary to perceive where the person lies along the Continuum of his or her type. In other words, one must assess whether a person is healthy, average, or unhealthy to understand the person properly. This is important because, for example, two people of the same type and wing will differ significantly if one is healthy and the other unhealthy. (In relationships and in the business world, understanding this distinction is crucial.)

The Continuum for each of the personality types can be seen in the following diagram. The Continuum is composed of nine internal Levels of Development. (Briefly, there are three Levels in the healthy section, three Levels in the average section, and three Levels in the unhealthy section.) It may help you to think of the Continuum as a photographer's gray scale which has gradations from pure white to pure black with many shades of gray in between. On the Continuum, the healthiest traits appear first, at the top, so to speak. As we regress down the Continuum we progressively pass through each Level of Development, marking a distinct shift in our personality's deterioration to the pure black of psychological breakdown at the bottom.

Healthy	Level 1
	Level 2
	Level 3
Average	Level 4
	Level 5
	Level 6
Unhealthy	Level 7
	Level 8
	Level 9

The Continuum of Traits

The Continuum helps make sense of each personality type as a whole by providing a framework on which to place each healthy, average, and unhealthy trait. The Continuum is also worth understanding because it is in the healthy range that we move in the Direction of Integration, just as it is in the average to unhealthy range that we "act out" in the Direction of Disintegration. It is worth noting that the Direction of Integration always involves conscious choice and effort, whereas the Direction of Disintegration is the path of least resistance and is the result of the habitual mechanisms of our personality. We can learn to be healthy just as, in different ways and for different reasons, we learn to be unhealthy. (For more, see *PT*, 41–42, 313–18; *UTE*, 89–119.)

Typing Yourself and Others

Once you have used the *Riso-Hudson Enneagram Type Indicator* to discover your type, you may be curious about the personality types of others. Since you will usually not be able to administer the RHETI to business associates or to strangers, you might wonder how you can become more skilled at discovering which type someone else is. By studying the descriptions in *Personality Types* and *Understanding the Enneagram*, you will in time become more adept at typing people. As you do so, you might keep several points in mind.

You may be able to figure out the types of a few close friends rather quickly, or you may find it difficult to identify people and not know where to begin. Either state is normal. It is not always apparent which type someone is, and it takes time and study to sharpen your skills. Remember that you are like a beginning medical student who is learning to diagnose a wide variety of conditions, some healthy, some unhealthy. It takes practice to learn to identify the various "symptoms" of each type and to see larger "syndromes."

Despite the subtleties and complexities involved, there is really no secret about typing people. You must learn which traits go with each type and observe how people manifest those traits. This is a subtle undertaking because there are many subtypes and quirks to each personality type. Different types can sometimes seem similar, particularly if their motivations are not taken into account. This is why it is not sufficient to focus on a single trait in isolation and make a diagnosis based on it alone. It is necessary to see each type as a whole — its overall style, approach to life, and especially its underlying motivations — before you can determine someone's type reliably. Many elements must come together before you can be sure that you have typed someone accurately.

Moreover, when we diagnose others, we are always on thinner ice than when we use the Enneagram to deepen our own self-knowledge. It is, of course, more appropriate to apply this material to ourselves than to type others while we avoid looking at our own lives. Nevertheless, it is unrealistic to think that anything as interesting (or as insightful) as the Enneagram will not be used to understand others. In fact, we categorize people all the time. No one approaches others without some sort of mental categories. We automatically perceive people either as male or female, attractive or unattractive, good or bad, friend or enemy, and so forth. It is simply honest to be aware of this. It is also useful to have more accurate and appropriate categories for everyone, including ourselves.

Although the Enneagram is probably the most open-ended and dynamic of typologies, this does not imply that the Enneagram can say all there is to say about human beings. Individuals are understandable only up to a certain point, beyond which they remain mysterious and unpredictable. Thus, while there can be no simple explanations for persons, it is still possible to say something true about them. In the last analysis, the Enneagram helps us to do that — and only that. The Enneagram is useful because it indicates with startling clarity certain constellations of meaning about something that is essentially beyond definition: the mystery that we are.

PART · TWO

SECTION 2. Instructions

THE *Riso-Hudson Enneagram Type Indicator* consists of 144 paired statements. It is a forced-choice test: it requires you to choose the statement in each pair that describes you best. In certain pairs, you may feel that neither describes you very well or, conversely, that both statements are almost equally true. Nevertheless, you must try to choose the statement that describes you *as you have been most of your life.*

Mark an X in the box to the right of the statement you have selected. For example, if you feel that a statement such as "I have preferred oranges" fits you better than "I have preferred apples," draw an X in the box to the right of the first statement. You may, of course, not have liked either oranges or apples, or you may have liked both. But if you were forced to choose between the two, which would you choose? Select the statement that reflects your lifelong attitudes and behavior better than the other. (If, for example, you have preferred apples most of your life but now prefer oranges, choose the apples statement.)

Be sure to choose one statement for each of the 144 pairs, taking care to put an X in the correct box. To help, a dotted line has been drawn from the end of each statement to its corresponding box in the columns on the right of the page.

You may find that there are five to ten pairs of statements for which the choice is particularly difficult. The statements in the RHETI are making subtle distinctions between the personality types, and choosing one over the other requires you to think carefully about which response is more true of you. In some of the pairs, both statements may *almost* be equally true. If you reflect carefully, however, you will find that one of the statements is more true than the other. Choose this statement in each pair.

Remember that there are no "right" answers. This instrument is attempting to discover your basic personality type, and if several of your selections are actually "wrong," they will not, in general, invalidate the test. So-called incorrect responses will more likely occur with factors other than those involving your basic personality type. This is why the degree of falsification they introduce in the test will be relatively small. To ensure the test's overall validity, however, it is essential that you answer honestly and thoughtfully, choosing the statement in each pair that accurately reflects your attitudes and feelings over most of your life. Optimally, you should choose one of the statements in all 144 pairs; however, if there are a few pairs in which you are absolutely certain that neither statement fits you, leave them blank. The RHETI is not attempting to ascertain whether or not you are healthy or unhealthy. A diagnosis such as this is beyond the scope of this test.

You may want to skip particularly difficult pairs and return to them after you have finished the entire test. Or you may wish to review your choices for the whole test after you have gone through it once. Feel free to change an original response if, after further reflection, you feel that another response is more appropriate. Naturally, you must guard against attempting to "fix" the results toward one type or another. But, because of nervousness, resistance, or other factors, you may not be able to answer some of the questions on a first pass through the test. If so, please review your responses.

The profile you get from the RHETI will reflect your personality's principal psychological functions, the balance of which changes over time. While your basic personality type will remain the same, other personality functions shift as you grow, deteriorate, change attitudes, experience stress, and so forth. You may find it informative to take the RHETI on several occasions to see what changes (if any) occur in your profile. If you have difficulty discovering your type because two or more top scores are very close, you might also find it helpful to discuss your choices with someone who knows you well, such as a spouse, close friend, or therapist. You may also ask someone else to take the RHETI for you as an external observer, answering the questions as he or she sees you. This approach, from the point of view of how others see us, can be particularly illuminating. Several scoring sheets have been provided at the end of the test (Section 4) so that you or others can take it on different occasions. Taking and grading the RHETI will require approximately one hour.

After you have taken the *Riso-Hudson Enneagram Type Indicator,* read the corresponding short Profiles of your type and wing provided in Section 5 to confirm your results. (Also see *Personality Types* and *Understanding the Enneagram* for more information and complete descriptions.)

Remember that the primary goal of this test is to determine your basic personality type; in some cases, it may be necessary to interpret the results to account for unusual findings. For guidelines about interpreting the RHETI, see Section 6. Again, remember to choose statements based on how you have felt and behaved *most of your life.*

Please note! The accuracy of this questionnaire will be increased if you understand that, in a sense, we have four "selves"—our past self, our present self, our ideal self, and our self as others see us. **The RHETI is attempting to discern only your past self.** It is therefore essential to maintain the focus of your answers *on your past self only,* and not to mix responses from your past self with your present, ideal, or social self. (The RHETI also includes several questions that ask us how we think or believe others see us. However, these questions should also be answered from the point of view of your past self.)

Naturally, if you have been in therapy, a psychological, or a spiritual practice of some kind, you will have changed. Nevertheless, your core self will remain the same since your basic personality type does not change. By responding to the statements as *you have been most of your life,* you will find out what your "core" self is.

SECTION 3. The Riso–Hudson Enneagram Type Indicator (Version 2.0)

	A	B	C	D	E	F	G	H	I
1. I've been romantic and imaginative					⊠				
I've been pragmatic and down-to-earth		( )							
2. I have tended to take on confrontations								⊠	
I have tended to avoid confrontations	( )								
3. I have typically been diplomatic, charming, and ambitious			(⊠)						
I have typically been direct, formal, and idealistic				( )					
4. I have tended to be focused and intense								( )	
I have tended to be spontaneous and fun-loving									⊠
	A	B	C	D	E	F	G	H	I
SUBTOTAL			1		1		1		1

28

	A	B	C	D	E	F	G	H	I

5. I have been a hospitable person and have enjoyed welcoming new friends into my life. . . . . ( )
   I have been a private person and have not mixed much with others. . . . . (X)

6. Generally, it's been easy to "get a rise" out of me. . . . . ( )
   Generally, it's been difficult to "get a rise" out of me. . . . . (X)

7. I've been more of a "street-smart" survivor. . . . . ( )
   I've been more of a "high-minded" idealist. . . . . (X)

8. I have needed to show affection to people . . . . ( )
   I have preferred to maintain a certain distance with people. . . . . (X)

9. When presented with a new experience, I've usually asked myself if it would be useful to me . . . . ( )
   When presented with a new experience, I've usually asked myself if it would be enjoyable . . . . (X)

	A	B	C	D	E	F	G	H	I
SUBTOTAL	1	0	1	1				1	1

	A	B	C	D	E	F	G	H	I
10. I have tended to focus too much on myself					☒				
I have tended to focus too much on others	( )								
11. Others have depended on my insight and knowledge								☒	
Others have depended on my strength and decisiveness									( )
12. I have come across as being too unsure of myself			( )						
I have come across as being too sure of myself				☒					
13. I have been more relationship-oriented than goal-oriented							( )		
I have been more goal-oriented than relationship-oriented				☒					
14. I have not been able to speak up for myself very well							( )		
I have been outspoken — I've said what others wished they had the nerve to say									☒
15. It's been difficult for me to stop considering alternatives and do something definite								( )	
It's been difficult for me to take it easy and be more flexible				☒					
	A	B	C	D	E	F	G	H	I
SUBTOTAL			1	2	1			1	1

	A	B	C	D	E	F	G	H	I
16. I have tended to be hesitant and procrastinating...		( )							
I have tended to be bold and domineering								(X)	
17. My reluctance to get too involved has gotten me into trouble with people...........	(X)								
My eagerness to have people depend on me has gotten me into trouble with them							( )		
18. Usually, I have been able to put my feelings aside to get the job done			( )						
Usually, I have needed to work through my feelings before I could act						(X)			
19. Generally, I've been methodical and cautious......			( )						
Generally, I've been adventurous and taken risks									(X)
20. I have tended to be a supportive, giving person who enjoys the company of others......							(X)		
I have tended to be a serious, reserved person who likes discussing issues				( )					
	A	B	C	D	E	F	G	H	I
SUBTOTAL	|				|	|	|		|

	A	B	C	D	E	F	G	H	I
21. I've often felt the need to be a "pillar of strength"							( )		
I've often felt the need to perform perfectly			(X)						
22. I've typically been interested in asking tough questions and maintaining my independence								(X)	
I've typically been interested in maintaining my stability and peace of mind	( )								
23. I've been too hard-nosed and skeptical			( )						
I've been too softhearted and sentimental						(X)			
24. I've often worried that I'm missing out on something better									(X)
I've often worried that if I let down my guard, someone will take advantage of me							( )		
25. My habit of being "stand-offish" has annoyed people						(X)			
My habit of telling people what to do has annoyed people				( )					
	A	B	C	D	E	F	G	H	I
SUBTOTAL			\		\	)		)	/

	A	B	C	D	E	F	G	H	I
26. Usually, when troubles have gotten to me, I have been able to "tune them out"	( )								
Usually, when troubles have gotten to me, I have treated myself to something I've enjoyed									(X)
27. I have depended on my friends and they have known that they can depend on me		( )							
I have not depended on people; I have done things on my own			(X)						
28. I have tended to be detached and preoccupied								(X)	
I have tended to be moody and self-absorbed					( )				
29. I have liked to challenge people and "shake them up"							(X)		
I have liked to comfort people and calm them down						( )			
30. I have generally been an outgoing, sociable person								(X)	
I have generally been an earnest, self-disciplined person				( )					
	A	B	C	D	E	F	G	H	I
SUBTOTAL			1				1	1	2

	A	B	C	D	E	F	G	H	I
31. I've usually been shy about showing my abilities		( )							
I've usually liked to let people know what I can do well			(X)						
32. Pursuing my personal interests has been more important to me than having comfort and security...........									( )
Having comfort and security has been more important to me than pursuing my personal interests.....................		(X)							
33. When I've had conflicts with others, I've tended to withdraw......................					(X)				
When I've had conflicts with others, I've rarely backed down							( )		
34. I have given in too easily and let others push me around.......		( )							
I have been too uncompromising and demanding with others					(X)				
35. I've been appreciated for my unsinkable spirit and great sense of humor...............									( )
I've been appreciated for my quiet strength and exceptional generosity.....................						(X)			
	A	B	C	D	E	F	G	H	I
SUBTOTAL		\	l	l	l	l			

	A	B	C	D	E	F	G	H	I
36. Much of my success has been due to my talent for making a favorable impression.			☒						
Much of my success has been achieved despite my lack of interest in developing "interpersonal skills".									( )
37. I've prided myself on my perseverance and common sense.		☒							
I've prided myself on my originality and inventiveness				( )					
38. Basically, I have been easygoing and agreeable.	☒								
Basically, I have been hard-driving and assertive							( )		
39. I have worked hard to be accepted and well liked			( )						
Being accepted and well liked has not been a high priority for me.					☒				
40. In reaction to pressure from others, I have become more withdrawn.								☒	
In reaction to pressure from others, I have become more aggressive.									( )
	A	B	C	D	E	F	G	H	I
SUBTOTAL	I	)	I	I				I	

	A	B	C	D	E	F	G	H	I

41. People have been interested in me because I've been outgoing, engaging, and interested in them . . . . ( )
People have been interested in me because I've been quiet, unusual, and deep. . . . . (X)

42. Duty and responsibility have been important values for me. . . . . ( )
Harmony and acceptance have been important values for me. . . . . (X)

43. I've tried to motivate people by making big plans and big promises . . . . (X)
I've tried to motivate people by pointing out the consequences of not following my advice . . . . ( )

44. I have seldom been emotionally demonstrative. . . . . ( )
I have often been emotionally demonstrative . . . . (X)

45. Dealing with details has not been one of my strong suits . . . . (X)
I have excelled at dealing with details. ( )

	A	B	C	D	E	F	G	H	I
SUBTOTAL	1				1	1	1		1

	A	B	C	D	E	F	G	H	I

46. More often, I have emphasized how different I am from my friends......................... ( )
More often, I have emphasized how much I have in common with my friends............... ⊠ (A)

47. When situations have gotten heated, I have tended to stay on the sidelines.................. ( )
When situations have gotten heated, I have tended to get right into the middle of things............................. ⊠ (G)

48. I have stood by my friends, even when they have been wrong......................... ⊠ (B)
I have not wanted to compromise what is right for friendship........................... ( )

49. I've been a well-meaning supporter.......................... ( )
I've been a highly motivated go-getter............................ ⊠ (C)

50. When troubled, I have tended to brood about my problems......................... ( )
When troubled, I have tended to find distractions for myself............................. ⊠ (I)

	A	B	C	D	E	F	G	H	I
SUBTOTAL	1		1				1		1

	A	B	C	D	E	F	G	H	I

51. Generally, I've had strong
convictions and a sense of
how things should be . . . . ⊠ (D)
Generally, I've had serious
doubts and have questioned
how things seemed to be . . . . ( )

52. I've created problems with
others by being too pessimistic
and complaining . . . . ( )
I've created problems with
others by being too bossy and
controlling . . . . ⊠

53. I have tended to act on my
feelings and let the "chips fall
where they may" . . . . ⊠
I have tended not to act on my
feelings lest they stir up more
problems . . . . ( )

54. Being the center of attention
has usually felt natural to me. . . . . ⊠
Being the center of attention
has usually felt strange
to me. . . . . ( )

55. I've been careful, and have
tried to prepare for unforeseen
problems . . . . ( )
I've been spontaneous, and
have preferred to improvise as
problems come up . . . . ⊠

	A	B	C	D	E	F	G	H	I
SUBTOTAL			\						

	A	B	C	D	E	F	G	H	I

56. I have gotten angry when others have not shown enough appreciation for what I have done for them . . . . ( )
I have gotten angry when others have not listened to what I have told them . . . . ( )

57. Being independent and self-reliant has been important to me . . . . ☒
Being valued and admired has been important to me . . . . ( )

58. When I've debated with friends, I've tended to press my arguments forcefully . . . . ( )
When I've debated with friends, I've tended to let things go to prevent hard feelings . . . . ☒

59. I have often been possessive of loved ones — I have had trouble letting them be . . . . ☒
I have often "tested" loved ones to see if they were really there for me . . . . ( )

	A	B	C	D	E	F	G	H	I
SUBTOTAL	1					1	1		

	A	B	C	D	E	F	G	H	I

60. Organizing resources and making things happen has been one of my major strengths . . . . ( ) [G]

Coming up with new ideas and getting people excited about them has been one of my major strengths . . . . [X] [I]

61. I've tended to be driven and very hard on myself . . . . ( ) [D]

I've tended to be too emotional and rather undisciplined . . . . [X] [E]

62. I have tried to keep my life fast-paced, intense, and exciting . . . . ( ) [I]

I have tried to keep my life regular, stable, and peaceful . . . . [X] [A]

63. I have felt uncomfortable leaving past commitments, so I have had difficulty making major life-changes . . . . ( ) [B]

I have felt uncomfortable making long-term commitments, so I have made major life-changes fairly easily . . . . [X] [C]

	A	B	C	D	E	F	G	H	I
SUBTOTAL	1		1	1					1

	A	B	C	D	E	F	G	H	I
64. I generally have tended to dwell on my feelings and to hold onto them for a long time					X				
I generally have tended to minimize my feelings and not pay very much attention to them									( )
65. I have provided many people with attention and nurturance							X		
I have provided many people with direction and motivation								( )	
66. I've been too serious and strict with myself				( )					
I've been too freewheeling and permissive with myself									X
67. I've been self-assertive and driven to excel				X					
I've been modest and have been happy to go at my own pace	( )								
68. I've been proud of my clarity and objectivity								( )	
I've been proud of my reliability and commitment		X							
	A	B	C	D	E	F	G	H	I
SUBTOTAL	1	)			1	1			1

	A	B	C	D	E	F	G	H	I

69. I have spent a lot of time looking inward — understanding my feelings has been important to me . . . . ⋈ (E)
I have not spent much time looking inward — getting things done has been important to me . . . . ( ) (I)

70. I have thought of myself as a sunny, casual person . . . . ⋈ (A)
I have thought of myself as a serious, dignified person. . . . . ( ) (D)

71. I've had an agile mind and boundless energy . . . . ( ) (I)
I've had a caring heart and deep dedication . . . . ⋈ (F)

72. I have pursued activities that had a substantial potential for reward and personal recognition . . . . ( ) (C)
I have been willing to give up reward and personal recognition if it meant doing work I was really interested in . . . . ⋈ (H)

73. Fulfilling social obligations has seldom been high on my agenda. . . . . ⋈ (E)
I have usually taken my social obligations very seriously . . . . ( ) (B)

	A	B	C	D	E	F	G	H	I
SUBTOTAL	1				2	1		1	

	A	B	C	D	E	F	G	H	I

74. In most situations I have preferred to take the lead.... In most situations, I have preferred to let someone else take the lead.................( )

Row 74: G — ☒; A — ( )

75. Over the years, my values and lifestyle have changed several times....................( ) Over the years, my values and lifestyle have remained fairly consistent ....

Row 75: C — ( ); D — ☒

76. Typically, I have not had much self-discipline .... Typically, I have not had much connection with people......................

Row 76: I — ( ); H — ☒

77. I have often felt too emotionally vulnerable to be around others .... I have often felt that my sacrifices have been taken for granted ....

Row 77: E — ☒; G — ( )

78. I have had a tendency to think of worst-case scenarios .... I have had a tendency to think that everything will work out for the best ....

Row 78: C — ( ); A — ☒

	A	B	C	D	E	F	G	H	I
SUBTOTAL	1		1	1			1	1	

	A	B	C	D	E	F	G	H	I

79. People have trusted me because I am confident and can look out for them. . . . . [H: ☒]
People have trusted me because I am fair and will do what is right . . . . [D: ( )]

80. Often, I have been so involved in my own projects that I have become isolated from others . . . . [H: ☒]
Often, I have been so involved with others that I have neglected my own projects . . . . [F: ( )]

81. When meeting someone new, I have usually been poised and self-contained. . . . . [C: ☒]
When meeting someone new, I have usually been chatty and entertaining. . . . . [I: ( )]

82. Generally speaking, I have tended to be pessimistic . . . . [E: ( )]
Generally speaking, I have tended to be optimistic . . . . [A: ☒]

83. I have preferred to inhabit my own little world . . . . [H: ☒]
I have preferred to let the world know I'm here . . . . [G: ( )]

	A	B	C	D	E	F	G	H	I
SUBTOTAL	1		1				1	2	

	A	B	C	D	E	F	G	H	I
84. I have often been troubled by nervousness, insecurity, and doubt		( )							
I have often been troubled by anger, perfectionism, and impatience				(X)					
85. I realize that I have often been too personal and intimate							( )		
I realize that I have often been too cool and aloof.			X						
86. I have lost out because I have not felt up to taking opportunities						( )			
I have lost out because I have pursued too many possibilities									X
87. I have tended to take a long time to get into action								( )	
I have tended to get into action quickly.				X					
88. I usually have had difficulty making decisions.		( )							
I seldom have had difficulty making decisions							X		
89. I have had a tendency to come on a little too strong with people						X			
I have had a tendency not to assert myself enough with people.	( )								
	A	B	C	D	E	F	G	H	I
SUBTOTAL		1	2		1	1			1

	A	B	C	D	E	F	G	H	I

90. Generally, I have gone out of my way to meet people and make connections . . . . [✗ in C]
    Generally, I have not gone out of my way to meet people and make connections . . . . ( ) [I]

91. When I've been unsure of what to do, I've often sought the advice of others. . . . . [✗ in C]
    When I've been unsure of what to do, I've tried different things to see what worked best for me. . . . . ( ) [I]

92. I have worried that I would be left out of others' activities. . . . . [✗ in G]
    I have worried that others' activities would distract me from what I had to do . . . . . . ( ) [D]

93. Typically, when I have gotten angry, I have told people off. . . . . ( ) [H]
    Typically, when I have gotten angry, I have become distant . . . . [✗ in C]

94. I've tended to have trouble falling asleep. . . . . ( ) [H]
    I've tended to fall asleep easily . . . . [✗ in A]

	A	B	C	D	E	F	G	H	I
SUBTOTAL	1	1	2			1			

	A	B	C	D	E	F	G	H	I

95. I have often tried to figure
out how I could get closer
to others . . . . **[X in column G]**
I have often tried to figure out
what others want from me . . . . **( ) [column B]**

96. I have usually been
measured, straight-talking,
and deliberate. . . . . **( ) [column G]**
I have usually been excitable,
fast-talking, and witty . . . . **[X in column I]**

97. Often, I have not spoken up
when I've seen others making
a mistake . . . . **[X in column E]**
Often, I have helped others
see that they are making a
mistake. . . . . **( ) [column D]**

98. During most of my life,
I have been a stormy person
who has had many volatile
feelings. . . . . **( ) [column I]**
During most of my life, I have
been a steady person in whom
"still waters run deep". . . . . **[X in column A]**

99. When I have disliked people,
I have usually tried hard to
stay cordial — despite my
feelings. . . . . **[X in column C]**
When I have disliked people,
I have usually let them know
it — one way or another . . . . **( ) [column B]**

	A	B	C	D	E	F	G	H	I
SUBTOTAL	1		1		1	1			1

	A	B	C	D	E	F	G	H	I

100. Much of my difficulty with people has come from my touchiness and taking everything too personally..... Much of my difficulty with people has come from my not caring about social conventions . . . .

       100. — E: ☒ ; I: ( )

101. My approach has been to jump in and rescue people . . . . My approach has been to show people how to help themselves

       101. — G: ( ) ; H: ☒

102. Generally, I have enjoyed "letting go" and pushing the limits . . . . Generally, I have not enjoyed losing control of myself very much. . . . .

       102. — I: ( ) ; D: ☒

103. I've been overly concerned with doing better than others. . I've been overly concerned with making things OK for others. . . . .

       103. — C: ☒ ; A: ( )

104. My thoughts have generally been speculative — involving my imagination and curiosity. . . . . My thoughts have generally been practical — just trying to keep things going . . . .

       104. — H: ☒ ; B: ( )

	A	B	C	D	E	F	G	H	I
SUBTOTAL			\	\	\		\	|	

	A	B	C	D	E	F	G	H	I

105. One of my main assets has been my ability to take charge of situations . . . . ( ) *(in column G)*
One of my main assets has been my ability to describe internal states . . . . ⊠ *(in column E)*

106. I have pushed to get things done correctly, even if it made people uncomfortable . . . . ⊠ *(in column D)*
I have not liked feeling pressured, so I have not liked pressuring anyone else . . . . ( ) *(in column A)*

107. I've often taken pride in how important I am in others' lives . . . . ( ) *(in column F)*
I've often taken pride in my gusto and openness to new experiences . . . . ⊠ *(in column I)*

108. I have perceived that I've often come across to others as presentable, even admirable . . . . ⊠ *(in column C)*
I have perceived that I've often come across to others as unusual, even odd . . . . ( ) *(in column H)*

109. I have mostly done what I had to do . . . . ( ) *(in column B)*
I have mostly done what I wanted to do . . . . ⊠ *(in column E)*

	A	B	C	D	E	F	G	H	I
SUBTOTAL			1	1	2				1

	A	B	C	D	E	F	G	H	I
110. I have usually enjoyed high-pressure, even difficult, situations							☒		
I have usually disliked being in high-pressure, even difficult, situations	( )								
111. I've been proud of my ability to be flexible — what's appropriate or important often changes			( )						
I've been proud of my ability to take a stand — I've been firm about what I believe in				☒					
112. My style has leaned toward spareness and austerity								☒	
My style has leaned toward excess and overdoing things									( )
113. My own health and well-being have suffered because of my strong desire to help others						( )			
My relationships have suffered because of my strong desire to attend to my personal needs					☒				
114. Generally speaking, I've been too open and naive	☒								
Generally speaking, I've been too wary and guarded		( )							
	A	B	C	D	E	F	G	H	I
SUBTOTAL	\			\	\		\	\	

	A	B	C	D	E	F	G	H	I
115. I have sometimes put people off by being too aggressive							X		
I have sometimes put people off by being too uptight				( )					
116. Being of service and attending to the needs of others has been a high priority for me						( )			
Finding alternative ways of seeing and doing things has been a high priority for me ...								X	
117. Typically, I have been even-tempered			X						
Typically, I have had strong changes of mood...............									( )
118. Situations that stir up deep, intense emotions have appealed to me						( )			
Situations that make me feel calm and at ease have appealed to me...............	X								
119. I have cared less about practical results than about pursuing my interests........								X	
I have been practical and have expected my work to have concrete results							( )		

	A	B	C	D	E	F	G	H	I
SUBTOTAL	1		1				1	2	

	A	B	C	D	E	F	G	H	I
120. I have had a deep need to belong			( )						
I have had a deep need to feel balanced.				☒					
121. In the past, I've probably insisted on too much closeness in my friendships.						( )			
In the past, I've probably kept too much distance in my friendships.		☒							
122. I've had a tendency to keep thinking about things from the past.					( )				
I've had a tendency to keep anticipating things I'm going to do									☒
123. I've tended to see people as intrusive and demanding.								( )	
I've tended to see people as disorganized and irresponsible				( )					
124. Generally, I have not had much confidence in myself.			( )						
Generally, I have had confidence only in myself.							☒		
125. I've probably been too passive and uninvolved	☒								
I've probably been too controlling and manipulative.						( )			
	A	B	C	D	E	F	G	H	I
SUBTOTAL	1		1	1			1		1

	A	B	C	D	E	F	G	H	I

126. I've frequently been stopped in my tracks by my self-doubt . . . . ( )
    I've rarely let self-doubt stand in my way . . . . ☒ (C)

127. Given a choice between something familiar and something new, I have usually chosen something new . . . . ☒ (I)
    I've generally chosen what I knew I already liked: why be disappointed with something I might not like? . . . . ( ) (C)

128. I have given a lot of physical contact to reassure others about how I feel about them . . . . ☒ (G)
    I have generally felt that real love does not depend on physical contact . . . . ( ) (D)

129. When I've needed to confront someone, I've often been too harsh and direct . . . . ☒ (G)
    When I've needed to confront someone, I've often "beaten around the bush" too much . . . . ( ) (C)

	A	B	C	D	E	F	G	H	I
SUBTOTAL			1			1	1		1

	A	B	C	D	E	F	G	H	I
130. I have been attracted to subjects that others would probably find disturbing, even frightening.								( )	
I have preferred not to spend my time dwelling on disturbing, frightening subjects. . . .	☒								
131. I have gotten into trouble with people by being too intrusive and interfering								( )	
I have gotten into trouble with people by being too evasive and uncommunicative.		☒							
132. I've worried that I don't have the resources to fulfill the responsibilities I've taken on							( )		
I've worried that I don't have the self-discipline to focus on what will really fulfill me									☒
133. Generally, I've been a highly intuitive, individualistic person.					☒				
Generally, I've been a highly organized, responsible person			( )						
134. Overcoming inertia has been one of my main problems	( )								
Being unable to slow down has been one of my main problems									☒
	A	B	C	D	E	F	G	H	I
SUBTOTAL	\	1			1				2

	A	B	C	D	E	F	G	H	I
135. When I've felt insecure, I've reacted by becoming arrogant and dismissive			( )						
When I've felt insecure, I've reacted by becoming defensive and argumentative		X							
136. I have generally been open-minded and willing to try new approaches								( )	
I have generally been self-revealing and willing to share my feelings with others						X			
137. I've presented myself to others as tougher than I am . . .								X	
I've presented myself to others as caring more than I really do							( )		
138. I usually have followed my conscience and reason.					( )				
I usually have followed my feelings and impulses									X
139. Serious adversity has made me feel hardened and resolute .			X						
Serious adversity has made me feel discouraged and resigned . .		( )							
140. I've usually made sure I had some kind of "safety net" to fall back on			( )						
I've usually chosen to depend on as little as possible								X	
	A	B	C	D	E	F	G	H	I
SUBTOTAL		1	1		1		1	1	1

	A	B	C	D	E	F	G	H	I

141. I've had to be strong for others, so I haven't had time to deal with my feelings and fears . . . . [G ⊠]

I've had difficulty coping with my feelings and fears, so it's been hard for me to be strong for others . . . . [E ( )]

142. I have often wondered why people focus on the negative when there is so much that's wonderful about life . . . . [A ⊠]

I have often wondered why people are so happy when so much in life is messed up . . . . [D ( )]

143. I have tried hard not to be seen as a selfish person . . . . [F ⊠]

I have tried hard not to be seen as a boring person . . . . [I ( )]

144. I have avoided intimacy when I feared I would be overwhelmed by people's needs and demands . . . . [H ( )]

I have avoided intimacy when I feared I would not be able to live up to people's expectations of me . . . . [C ( )]

	A	B	C	D	E	F	G	H	I
SUBTOTAL	1				1	1			

SECTION 4. Scoring Instructions

ADD the X's marked in column A, column B, column C, and so forth, through column I, and enter the numbers in the corresponding boxes below. If you have marked one box in each pair of statements and have added the number of X's correctly, the sum will be 144. If not, go back and recheck for mistakes either in counting X's or in arithmetic. Each column corresponds to a personality type, as given in the chart below. Please note that the types have been randomized and are *not* in numerical order.

Columns	A	B	C	D	E	F	G	H	I
Numerical Value	17	7	21	13	19	13	17	14	20
Personality Type	Nine	Six	Three	One	Four	Two	Eight	Five	Seven

Mark the numerical value for each personality type on the score sheet on page 59. Note that the personality types have been arranged on the score sheet *in numerical order* beginning with types Two, Three, Four (in the Feeling Triad), and so forth. You may wish to connect the marks you have made to produce a graph.

Except in unusual circumstances (some of which are discussed in Section 6), your highest score will indicate your *basic personality type* — which is the object of this test. To confirm your test results, read the short Profile of your basic type in Section 5 as well as the more complete descriptions in *Personality Types* and *Understanding the Enneagram*.

An alternative method for discovering your personality type is to have one or more people who know you well take the RHETI as if they were answering the test for you (as mentioned in Section 2). This method tests how others see you; if their results and yours are the same (at least for the basic type), you can be reassured that the RHETI has discriminated your type accurately. On the other hand, a finding of a different basic type (or of a dramatically different pattern for the other eight types) could be the basis for discussing various dimensions of your personality that you formerly may have been unaware of.

The median score is 16 for each type. If the Functions of your personality were in perfect balance, you would score 16 on each of the nine types. This result is probably extremely rare, and it is normal to have wide variations from the median. Some scores will fall below the median, some will be above it. These variations produce a profile of your personality that represents your ever-changing responses to life. The "above average" and "below average" as well as the "high" and "low" ranges indicated on the score sheets are therefore not to be interpreted as indications of pathology or as value judgments. They are only indicators of the *relative* development of the various Functions within your personality. Thus, those Functions that are already developed probably do not need to be emphasized further, while you may want to give more attention to those with lower scores.

After you have plotted your scores on the score sheet(s), read the appropriate brief Profile of your type in Section 5 and then go to Section 6 for more information about interpreting your results.

Score Sheet I

Type	Two	Three	Four	Five	Six	Seven	Eight	Nine	One	
Score										
32										
31										
30										
29										
28										
27										
26										
25										
24										High
23										
22										
21		●								
20						●				Above
19			●							Average
18										
17							●	●		Median
16										
15				●						
14										
13	●								●	
12										Low
11										Average
10										
9										
8										Low
7					●					
6										
5										
4										
3										
2										
1										
0										
	Two	Three	Four	Five	Six	Seven	Eight	Nine	One	
	The Feeling Triad			The Doing Triad			The Relating Triad			

Score Sheet II

Type	Two	Three	Four	Five	Six	Seven	Eight	Nine	One	
Score										
32										
31										
30										
29										
28										
27										
26										
25										
24										High
23										
22										
21										
20										Above
19										Average
18										
17										
16										Median
15										
14										
13										
12										Below
11										Average
10										
9										
8										Low
7										
6										
5										
4										
3										
2										
1										
0										
	Two	Three	Four	Five	Six	Seven	Eight	Nine	One	
	The Feeling Triad			The Doing Triad			The Relating Triad			

Score Sheet III

Type	Two	Three	Four	Five	Six	Seven	Eight	Nine	One	
Score										
32										
31										
30										
29										
28										
27										
26										
25										
24										High
23										
22										
21										
20										Above
19										Average
18										
17										
16										Median
15										
14										
13										
12										Below
11										Average
10										
9										
8										Low
7										
6										
5										
4										
3										
2										
1										
0										
	Two	Three	Four	Five	Six	Seven	Eight	Nine	One	
	The Feeling Triad			The Doing Triad			The Relating Triad			

Score Sheet IV

Type	Two	Three	Four	Five	Six	Seven	Eight	Nine	One	
Score
32
31
30
29
28
27
26
25
24										High
23
22
21
20										Above
19										Average
18
17
16										Median
15
14
13
12										Below
11										Average
10
9
8										Low
7
6
5
4
3
2
1
0
	Two	Three	Four	Five	Six	Seven	Eight	Nine	One	
	The Feeling Triad			The Doing Triad			The Relating Triad			

PART·THREE

5. The Personality Types in Profile

Profiles

Now that you have discovered your personality type, you will naturally want to know more about what it means.

The following Profiles will introduce you to each of the nine personality types of the Enneagram. Remember that these Profiles are intentionally brief, impressionistic sketches and by no means exhaust the behaviors and motivations that make up each type, much less the insights that can be had about them.

Each Profile begins with a short overview of the type, then lists some of the major healthy, average, and unhealthy traits, and ends with references to *Personality Types* and *Understanding the Enneagram*. These books contain a wealth of information about each type, including full systematic descriptions, short profiles (in *PT*), expanded profiles (in *UTE*), descriptions of each type's Directions of Integration and Disintegration, its basic fear, basic desire, and secondary motivations, its developmental childhood origins, descriptions of the wings, examples of famous people (listed according to their wing), the type's sense of self, characteristic temptation, saving grace, characteristic vice and virtue, suggestions for personal growth, its abstract structural patterns, and much else. By my convention, the profiles begin with personality type Two in the Feeling Triad.

Personality Type Two: *The Helper*
The Caring, Nurturing Type: Concerned, Generous, Possessive,
and Manipulative

Personality type Two is the type in the Feeling Triad that is
overexpressive of its feelings. Twos demonstrate their emotions,
openly declaring their love and affection for others. The problem
is that while they are aware of their positive feelings for others,
they are unaware of many repressed negative feelings — such as
resentment and hostility — as well as their own needs and demands. Twos see themselves as loving, kind, and thoughtful (and
when they are healthy, they are). However, as they become unhealthy, their behavior contradicts their all-loving self-image as
they desperately coerce signs of love and appreciation from others. The following are some of the major behavioral characteristics of Twos.

Healthy: They are empathetic, compassionate, feeling with and
for others, caring and concerned about their needs. Encouraging,
appreciative, sincere, and warm-hearted. Service is very important to Twos: they are generous, giving, and helpful — loving,
thoughtful people. *At their best:* Very healthy Twos become
deeply unselfish, humble, and altruistic, giving unconditional
love to themselves and others. They feel it is a privilege to be in
the lives of others. They are saintly, radiant, and joyful — truly
healing presences in the world.

Average: Average Twos begin to do more talking about what they
will do for others than giving actual help. They become overly
friendly, emotionally demonstrative, histrionic, and full of "good
intentions" about everything. The attention they give is seduc-
tive: approval, "strokes," flattery, cultivating people. Love and
friendship are their supreme values, and they talk about them
constantly. Become overly intimate and intrusive: they need to
be needed, so they hover, meddle, and control in the name of
love. Wanting others to depend on them, they give but expect a
return. Enveloping and possessive — the self-sacrificial, smoth-

ering person who cannot do enough for others. They wear themselves out for everyone, creating needs for themselves to fulfill. They develop hypochondria, becoming "martyrs" for others. Feel increasingly self-important and indispensable, although they overrate their efforts in others' behalf. Overbearing, patronizing, and self-satisfied.

Unhealthy: They can be manipulative and guilt-instilling while abusing food and medication to "stuff" their feelings. Undermine people, making belittling, disparaging remarks. Extremely self-deceptive about their motives and about how aggressive or selfish their behavior has become. Domineering and coercive, they feel entitled to get anything they want from others — the repayment of old debts, money, sexual favors. Able to excuse and rationalize whatever they do since they feel abused and victimized and are bitterly resentful and angry. The chronic suppression of their aggressions results in severe health problems.

See *Personality Types*, 49–76, *Understanding the Enneagram*, 44–49, and "Recommendations for Personal Growth" in *UTE*, 236–38.

Personality Type Three: *The Motivator*
The Success-Oriented, Pragmatic Type: Adaptable, Ambitious, Image-Conscious, and Hostile

Personality type Three is the type in the Feeling Triad that is most out of touch with its feelings. Thus, the underlying problem with average to unhealthy Threes is that they tend to disown their true self to become more acceptable to others. They have put their energy primarily into learning how to come across well so that they can garner attention and admiration. Threes have learned to do what it takes to be noticed and to be in demand socially by projecting a desirable image. Because their private sense of self remains undeveloped, however, average to unhealthy Threes do not know who they are apart from the images they project. Rather than express what they actually think or feel, they say or do what will be acceptable and applauded. Some of the major behavioral characteristics of Threes are the following.

Healthy: They are self-assured, desirable, have high self-esteem, and believe in themselves and their own value. Adaptable, energetic, often physically attractive and popular. Ambitious to improve themselves, to be the best they can be: they often become outstanding, a human ideal, embodying widely admired cultural qualities. Others are motivated to be like them in some positive way. *At their best:* Self-accepting, inner-directed, and authentic, everything they seem to be. They accept their limitations and live within them: modest and touchingly honest themselves.

Average: They become highly concerned with their performance, doing the job well, and being effective, often comparing self with others in search of success and status. They become careerists, determined to distinguish themselves in some way: achievement and social recognition are important. Pragmatic, goal-oriented, and efficient, but also calculating, becoming image-conscious, highly aware of how they appear to others. Potential problems with intimacy and honesty emerge as they package the self according to the expectations of others, doing whatever produces the desired results. As identification with performance increases, they want to impress others and have their image reinforced. They constantly promote themselves, inflating their importance and accomplishments. Narcissistic, pretentious, with grandiose ideas about themselves. Aggression and competitiveness, as well as arrogance, hostility, and contempt for others surface.

Unhealthy: Desperately fearing failure and humiliation, they can be exploitative and opportunistic. To maintain their position on top, they may use others dishonestly, lie, or steal (things, ideas, corporate information, and so on). Devious and deceptive to conceal their mistakes and wrongdoings, they will go to great lengths to convince others that they are still a "winner." Delusionally jealous of others, becoming vindictive and attempting to ruin others. Relentless and obsessive, psychopathic tendencies emerge as extreme form of pathology.

See *Personality Types*, 77–104, *Understanding the Enneagram*, 49–53, and "Recommendations for Personal Growth" in *UTE*, 239–41.

Personality Type Four: *The Artist*
The Sensitive, Withdrawn Type: Intuitive, Individualistic, Self-Absorbed, and Depressive

Personality type Four is the type in the Feeling Triad that under-expresses its feelings. Fours find their feelings difficult to express because they are powerful, mixed with sexual and forbidden elements, often including hostile thoughts about themselves and others. Because their feelings can be shameful, chaotic, and "dangerous," average to unhealthy Fours have learned to keep their feelings to themselves, partly so that they can sort them out, and partly to spare themselves from humiliation or punishment if they were to reveal how they actually feel. But as they continue to turn their feelings inward, average to unhealthy Fours become painfully self-conscious and emotionally vulnerable and suffer many far-ranging practical negative consequences in their lives and relationships. Some of the major behavioral characteristics of Fours are the following.

Healthy: Fours are self-aware, introspective, emotionally strong, aware of feelings and inner impulses. Intuitive and sensitive both to self and others: gentle, tactful, compassionate. Ironic view of life and self: can be serious and funny, finding humor in their own foibles. Highly personal, individualistic, true to self, self-revealing, emotionally honest, and humane. *At their best:* Profoundly creative, expressing the personal and the universal, possibly in art. Inspired, self-renewing, and regenerative: able to transform all their experiences into something valuable for others as well.

Average: They take an artistic, aesthetic, romantic orientation to life, expressing personal feelings through something beautiful. Reinforce their sense of self through fantasy and the imagination. To stay in touch with feelings, they interiorize everything, taking everything personally, becoming self-absorbed, introverted, and moody. Also become hypersensitive, shy and very self-conscious, unable to be spontaneous or to get outside themselves. They remain socially withdrawn to protect the vulnerable self and to sort out their mixed, increasingly negative feelings. They gradually feel different from others and therefore exempt from living as others do. Self-pity leads to self-indulgence, to becoming melancholic dreamers, disdainful, decadent and sensual, living in a fantasy world that repels any kind of pressure or intrusion. Increasingly temperamental, impractical, unproductive, effete, and petulant.

Unhealthy: When their dreams and expectations fail, they become angry at themselves: self-inhibited, depressed, alienated, incapacitated, blocked, and emotionally paralyzed. Ashamed of self, fatigued, and unable to function. Tormented by delusional self-contempt, self-hatred, and morbid thoughts: everything adds to their self-reproach. They despair, feel hopeless, and become self-destructive, possibly abusing alcohol or drugs to escape. In the extreme, crimes of passion or suicide are the likely forms of pathology.

See *Personality Types,* 105–33, *Understanding the Enneagram,* 53–57, and "Recommendations for Personal Growth" in *UTE,* 241–44.

Personality Type Five: *The Thinker*
The Intense, Cerebral Type: Perceptive, Original, Provocative, and Eccentric

Personality type Five is the type in the Doing Triad that has underdeveloped its ability to do or to take practical action. Fives tend to substitute thinking for doing, feeling that they cannot risk acting until they have first carefully thought about what they might do, learned as much as possible about the task at hand, and foreseen every possible outcome if they act one way or another. Fives are caught in their heads, in thinking, since thinking about doing, feelings, and relationships is safer and less threatening than experiencing them. Fives are constantly preparing themselves, acquiring expertise in some area that will give them confidence and a niche in the world. The following are some of their major behavioral characteristics.

Healthy: They observe everything with extraordinary perceptiveness and insight. Mentally alert, curious, with a searching intelligence: nothing escapes their notice. They value foresight and prediction. Able to concentrate, becoming engrossed in what has caught their attention. They attain mastery of whatever interests them. Independent, innovative, inventive, producing extremely valuable, original works. *At their best:* Become visionaries, broadly comprehending the world while penetrating it profoundly. Open-minded, take things in whole, in their true context. Make pioneering discoveries of something entirely new.

Average: They begin conceptualizing everything — working things out in their minds: model building, preparing, practicing, gathering more resources and techniques. Often "intellectual," into building theories. Detachment increases as they get drawn into complicated ideas and imaginary worlds — fascinated by offbeat, esoteric subjects, even those involving dark and disturbing elements. They act like they are "disembodied minds," more preoccupied with their visions and interpretations than reality, becoming high-strung and intense. They begin to take an antagonistic stance toward anything that interferes with their inner world and personal vision. They become provocative and abrasive with intentionally extreme and radical views. Cynical and argumentative.

Unhealthy: They become reclusive and isolated, eccentric and nihilistic. Highly unstable and fearful of aggressions: reject and repulse all social attachments, becoming eccentric, strange.

Frightened by threatening ideas, yet obsessed by them as well: they become horrified, paranoid, and are prey to gross distortions and phobias. Eventually break with reality: insanity with schizophrenic tendencies is the likely form of pathology.

See *Personality Types*, 134–61, *Understanding the Enneagram*, 58–62, and "Recommendations for Personal Growth" in *UTE*, 244–46.

Personality Type Six: *The Loyalist*
The Committed, Security-Oriented Type: Engaging, Responsible, Defensive, and Paranoid

Personality type Six is the type in the Doing Triad that is most out of touch with its ability to act independently of others. People of this type have little or no problem with doing; however, they tend to distrust their own thoughts and decisions and so look for others whom they can trust and depend on. Sixes invest their time and energy in people and groups that offer security and safety, but they also feel suspicious that others — including allies — will take advantage of them. Average to unhealthy Sixes are prey to anxiety and insecurity when they are unsure of where they stand with others, particularly with their allies and supporters. Some of the major behavioral characteristics of Sixes are the following.

Healthy: Sixes are able to elicit strong emotional responses from others: can be very appealing, endearing, and lovable. Trust is important: bonding with others, forming permanent relationships. Committed and loyal to those with whom they have identified: family and friends are important, as is the sense that they belong somewhere. Respond with reliable, responsible, trustworthy behavior. *At their best:* They become self-affirming, trusting of self and others, independent yet symbiotically interdependent and cooperative as an equal. Faith in self leads to courage, positive thinking, leadership, and rich self-expression, sometimes as an artist.

Average: They fear taking responsibility for themselves: prefer implementing well-defined rules and structures. They identify strongly with whatever gives them security. Traditionalistic and loyal to those they have bonded with, working for stability and continuity. However, they may also react against their allies indirectly, passive-aggressively. Feeling pressured by responsibilities, they become evasive, indecisive, cautious, suspicious, and defensive. Increasingly contradictory, they give mixed signals and react unpredictably. To overcompensate for insecurities, they become mean-spirited and belligerent, taking an aggressive stance toward anyone they perceive as an enemy or threat to them and their security. In-groups and out-groups are identified, as they become highly partisan, looking for scapegoats. Authoritarian, prejudiced, and fear-instilling to silence their own fears.

Unhealthy: Fearing that they have ruined their security, unhealthy Sixes become neurotically insecure, clingingly dependent, and self-disparaging, with acute inferiority feelings. Feel hopeless, worthless, incompetent. Extremely anxious, they feel persecuted and believe that others are out to get them. They lash out and act irrationally, ironically bringing about what they fear. Sixes may turn to extreme forms of substance abuse, fanatical beliefs, or violence to avoid the consequences of their actions. Hysterical and seeking to escape punishment, they can become self-destructive and suicidal.

See *Personality Types*, 162–89, *Understanding the Enneagram*, 63–67, and "Recommendations for Personal Growth," in *UTE*, 247–49.

Personality Type Seven: *The Generalist*
The Spontaneous, Busy Type: Enthusiastic, Accomplished, Excessive, and Manic

Personality type Seven is the type in the Doing Triad that has overdeveloped its ability to do. People of this type tend to do too much: they put few restraints on themselves as they constantly search for new experiences and sources of stimulation. Average to unhealthy Sevens often have many varied experiences and yet are unsatisfied because they cannot focus themselves on anything (lest they miss out on something more desirable). They impulsively do too many things at the same time, distracting themselves by acquiring and consuming more of everything to deaden anxiety and spare themselves from the fear of being deprived. Some of the major behavioral characteristics of Sevens are the following.

Healthy: They are highly responsive, excitable, enthusiastic, the most extroverted type: stimuli bring immediate responses, and they find everything invigorating. Lively, vivacious, eager, spontaneous, resilient, exhilarated. Quickly become accomplished achievers who do many things well: they are multitalented generalists. Practical, highly productive, prolific, cross-fertilizing their many areas of interest and skills. *At their best:* They assimilate experiences in depth, making them deeply grateful and appreciative, awed by the wonders of life: joyous and ecstatic. They have intimations of spiritual reality, of the boundless goodness of life.

Average: They begin pursuing a wider range of experiences that they believe will satisfy them. Become acquisitive and worldly-wise, constantly seeking new things and experiences: the sophisticate, connoisseur, collector, and consumer. Being free and keeping their options open are important. Become hyperactive, unable to say no to themselves, to deny themselves anything. Uninhibited, they throw themselves into constant activity, doing and saying whatever comes to mind: flamboyant exaggerations, storytelling, wisecracking constantly. Distracted and scattered, they begin to squander their time and energy. Fear being bored: in perpetual motion, but into too many things, becoming superficial dilettantes merely dabbling around. Materialistic, they get into conspicuous consumption and become excessive, yet greedy for more, never feeling that they have enough. Demanding, self-centered, yet jaded and unsatisfied. Hardened and insensitive, with addictive tendencies.

Unhealthy: They can be offensive and abusive while going after what they want. Impulsive and infantile, not knowing when to stop. Addictions and excess take their toll: they become debauched, dissipated escapists. Desperately acting out impulses rather than dealing with anxiety or frustrations, they go out of control, into erratic mood swings and compulsive actions (manias). In flight from self, subject to panic reactions if defenses fail. Severe manic-depressive mood swings are the likely form of pathology.

See *Personality Types*, 190–217, *Understanding the Enneagram*, 67–71, and "Recommendations for Personal Growth" in *UTE*, 249–51.

Personality Type Eight: *The Leader*
The Powerful, Dominating Type: Self-Confident, Decisive, Confrontational, and Ruthless

Personality type Eight is the type in the Relating Triad that has overdeveloped its ability to relate to and dominate the environment. Eights typically have problems being close with people because they fear that others will try to control them. They see themselves as people who can get what they want. While not necessarily brutal, Eights can be aggressive in an unstated fight for survival for themselves and for those they are protecting and defending. They can have either a highly beneficial effect on the environment or just the reverse. Some of the major behavioral characteristics of Eights are the following.

Healthy: Eights are self-assertive, self-confident, and strong: they have learned to stand up for what they need and want. Have a resourceful, can-do attitude and inner drive. Decisive, solid, authoritative, commanding, honorable: natural leaders, whom others look up to. Passionate, they take initiative and make things happen: champion of people, provider, protector. *At their best:* Become self-restrained and magnanimous, merciful and forbearing, mastering self, carrying others with their strength. Courageous, willing to put themselves in jeopardy to achieve their vision: possibly heroic and historically great.

Average: Self-sufficiency, independence, and having enough resources are important concerns, so they become enterprising, pragmatic, "rugged individualists" and wheeler-dealers. Adventurous, risk-taking, and hard-working, but deny their own emotional vulnerability. They begin to dominate their environment, including others: want to feel that others are behind them, supporting their efforts. Boastful, forceful, and expansive, they see themselves as the "boss" whose word is law. Proud and egocentric, they resist control by imposing their will on others, not treating them as equals. Everything becomes a test of wills, and they will not back down. Eights create adversarial relationships, becoming confrontational, combative, and intimidating. They use threats and reprisals to get obedience and to keep potential opponents off balance. However, their unjust treatment may cause others to band against them.

Unhealthy: Defying any attempt by others to control them, they can be completely ruthless and dictatorial, believing that "might makes right." Hardhearted, immoral, and violent. Develop delusional ideas about themselves: megalomaniacal, omnipotent, invulnerable. They recklessly overextend themselves, and if in danger, they may brutally destroy everything rather than surrender to anyone else. Pathology is extreme antisocial behavior: vengeful, barbaric, murderous.

See *Personality Types*, 218–45, *Understanding the Enneagram*, 72–76, and "Recommendations for Personal Growth" in *UTE*, 252–54.

Personality Type Nine: *The Peacemaker*
The Easygoing, Self-Effacing Type: Accepting, Reassuring, Passive, and Repressed

Personality type Nine is the type in the Relating Triad that is most out of touch with its ability to relate to the environment as it is. People of this type have so completely identified with an idealized vision of reality or another person that they lack a sufficient sense of themselves apart from their idealizations. Nines and their idealized visions merge into one. While this gives Nines a profound sense of peace and well-being, it also causes them to be too repressed, undeveloped, and unresponsive to reality. Rather than deal with anything that upsets them or contradicts their idealized vision, average to unhealthy Nines ignore what they do not want to see. The following are some of the major behavioral characteristics of Nines.

Healthy: They are deeply accepting, receptive, unself-conscious, emotionally stable and serene. Nines are trusting of self and others, at ease with life and the natural world. Patient, unpretentious, genuinely good-natured people. Optimistic, reassuring, supportive: a calming influence — harmonizing groups, bringing people together. Good mediator, synthesizer, communicator. *At their best:* They become self-possessed, feeling autonomous and fulfilled: have great equanimity and contentment. Paradoxically independent, at one with self, and thus able to form profound relationships. More alive, awake, alert to self and others. Truly accepting, yet powerfully involved with life.

Average: They become self-effacing, accommodating themselves, idealizing others and going along with their wishes too much, living through them. Accept conventional roles and expectations naively, unquestioningly. Fearing change and conflicts, they become passive and disengaged: too easygoing, unresponsive, complacent, and phlegmatic, they walk away from problems, brushing them under the rug. Thinking becomes hazy and ruminative, mostly about their fantasies, as they begin to tune out reality, becoming oblivious, unreflective, and inattentive. Emotional indolence, indifference, unwillingness to exert self (and stay focused) on problems when the need arises. Begin to minimize problems to appease others and to have peace at any price. Become fatalistic and resigned, as if nothing can be done to change anything. Engage in wishful thinking, looking for quick, magical solutions.

Unhealthy: They can become repressed, undeveloped, and ineffectual. Do not want to deal with problems: obstinate, dissociating self from all conflicts. Thus, they become neglectful and dangerous to others. Dissociate so much from anything threatening that they eventually cannot function: severely disoriented, depersonalized, catatonic. Multiple personalities are possible as extreme pathology.

See *Personality Types*, 246–73, *Understanding the Enneagram*, 76–81, and "Recommendations for Personal Growth" in *UTE*, 255–57.

Personality Type One: *The Reformer*
The Rational, Idealistic Type: Principled, Orderly, Perfectionistic, and Self-Righteous

Personality type One is the type in the Relating Triad whose ability to relate to the environment is restricted; that is, Ones need to feel justified by their conscience before they can act. Ones also have problems relating to people and the environment because they see themselves as needing to be perfect before they allow themselves to do whatever they do or want whatever they want. Ones see themselves and the world around them as being in less than an ideal state; hence, they are unsatisfied with reality as it is (and with themselves) since the world could always be improved. Average to unhealthy Ones become increasingly angry and intolerant if the environment does not obey their prescriptions for perfection. Some of the major behavioral characteristics of Ones are the following.

Healthy: They are conscientious with strong personal convictions. Rational, reasonable, self-disciplined, mature, moderate. Extremely principled, always want to be fair and objective with others. Ethical: truth and justice are primary values. A sense of higher purpose and personal integrity make them teachers and witnesses to the truth. *At their best:* They become extraordinarily wise, discerning, and humane. Transcendentally realistic, accepting themselves and reality as they are. Inspiring and hopeful, they believe that the truth will eventually be heard.

Average: They become high-minded idealists, feeling *noblesse oblige* — that it is up to them to strive to improve everything: reformers, advocates, critics, and crusaders. They become involved in causes, making progress toward the ideal, toward how they think things "ought" to be. Afraid of making a mistake: everything must be consistent with their ideals. Become orderly and well organized but impersonal, too emotionally constricted, rigid and logical, keeping their feelings and impulses in tight check. Puritanical, punctual, pedantic, and fastidious. Their thinking is deductive and hierarchical, in dichotomies of black and white, right and wrong, good and bad. Very critical both of self and others: picky, judgmental, perfectionistic. Highly opinionated about everything: correcting people and badgering them to do what they think is right. Impatient, never settling for less than perfection in self and others. Moralizing, scolding, abrasive, and indignantly angry toward people if they do not do as they are told.

Unhealthy: They can be highly dogmatic, self-righteous, intolerant, and inflexible. Unhealthy Ones deal in absolutes: they alone know "the truth." Very severe in judgments toward others, although rationalizing their own actions. While obsessed about the wrongdoing of others, Ones may become contradictory and hypocritical, doing the opposite of what they preach. Become condemnatory, punitive, and cruel. Pathology seen as a serious nervous breakdown and severe depression.

See *Personality Types,* 274–301, *Understanding the Enneagram,* 81–85, and "Recommendations for Personal Growth" in *UTE,* 258–60.

SECTION 6. Interpreting the RHETI

$\mathbb{A}$LTHOUGH discovering your basic personality type is the primary objective of the RHETI, you can also gain more information about your personality and its dynamics from the test.

In most cases, the highest score is your basic personality type; however, occasionally the basic type may be only two or three points higher than another type, or several types may be equal. There may also be other unusual results. This section is concerned with interpreting the RHETI, particularly in cases where the results are somewhat ambiguous.

In this section, we will discuss the nine personality types as psychological Functions operative within each of us, briefly comment on patterns and issues frequently seen with this questionnaire, and present five case studies that illustrate different aspects of interpretation.

The Functions

From one point of view, each of the personality types is a metaphor for a wide range of behaviors and attitudes, just as in astrology different "houses" denote particular areas of human activity. The nine personality types of the Enneagram can thus be regarded as psychological "functions" and "potentials for" a wide spectrum of healthy to unhealthy traits. One reason we are all similar is that all nine Functions operate in each of us; one reason we are different is that their proportion and balance within our psyches is different.

I have given two names to each Function because each personality type represents two major areas of activity — a Function that characterizes an internally held *attitude* of the type and a Function that characterizes the type's observable *behavior.* High scores in one or more of the types indicate that you have already developed the Functions or the capacities of these types, whereas relatively low scores indicate that you might want to give more attention to developing these other potentials. (The following short sketches of the Functions are suggestive, not exhaustive, treatments of this aspect of the Enneagram. For more qualities associated with each type as a Function, read the descriptions provided in *Personality Types* and *Understanding the Enneagram* with this interpretation in mind.)

Understood as a series of interrelated psychological Functions, the nine personality types of the Enneagram reveal the full range of one's personality. The balance of the Functions in each person produces that person's distinctive "fingerprint" or "signature": while the basic type remains dominant, the other Functions in the overall pattern change over time.

Looked at from the viewpoint of the Functions, our basic personality type can thus be seen for what it is — a dominant Function (a mode of being) around which we have organized our central response to reality — while the other eight types represent the wide range of potentials that also exist within us.

THE FEELING TRIAD

TYPE TWO. The Functions of *Empathy* and *Altruism:* the potential for other-directedness, thoughtfulness for others, genuine self-sacrifice, generosity, and nurturance. Negatively, the potential for intrusiveness, possessiveness, manipulation, and self-deception.

TYPE THREE. The Functions of *Self-Esteem* and *Self-Development:* The potential for self-improvement, personal excellence, professional competence, self-assurance, ambition, and social distinction. Negatively, the potential for pragmatic calculation, arrogant narcissism, grandiosity, and hostility.

TYPE FOUR. The Functions of *Self-Awareness* and *Artistic Creativity:* The potential for intuition, sensitivity, individualism, self-expression, and self-revelation. Negatively, the potential for self-absorption, self-consciousness, self-doubt, and self-inhibition.

THE DOING TRIAD

TYPE FIVE. The Functions of *Open-Mindedness* and *Original Thinking:* The potential for curiosity, perceptiveness, the acquisition of knowledge, inventive originality, and technical expertise. Negatively, the potential for speculative theorizing, emotional detachment, eccentricity, and social isolation.

TYPE SIX. The Functions of *Commitment* and *Social Affiliation:* The potential for creating security, for cooperation, sociability, industriousness, loyalty to others, and sacrifice for larger efforts. Negatively, the potential for dependency, suspicion, belligerence, and inferiority feelings.

TYPE SEVEN. The Functions of *Enthusiasm* and *Practical Action:* The potential for responsiveness, productivity, achievement, skill acquisition, and the desire for change and variety. Negatively, the potential for hyperactivity, superficiality, impulsiveness, excessiveness, and escapism.

THE RELATING TRIAD

TYPE EIGHT. The Functions of *Self-Assertion* and *Leadership:* The potential for self-confidence, self-determination, self-reliance, magnanimity, and the ability to take personal initiative. Negatively, the potential for domination of others, insensitivity, combativeness, and ruthlessness.

TYPE NINE. The Functions of *Acceptance* and *Receptivity:* The potential for emotional stability, humility, unself-consciousness, emotional and physical endurance, and creating harmony with others. Negatively, the potential for passivity, disengaged emotions and attention, neglectfulness, and mental dissociation.

TYPE ONE. The Functions of *Objectivity* and *Social Responsibility:* The potential for moderation, conscience, maturity, self-discipline, and delayed gratification. Negatively, the potential for rigid self-control, impersonal perfectionism, judgmentalism, and self-righteousness.

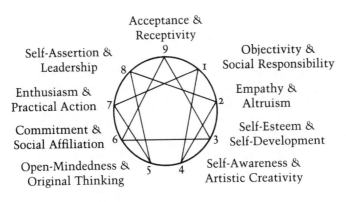

Acceptance &
Receptivity

Self-Assertion &
Leadership

Objectivity &
Social Responsibility

Enthusiasm &
Practical Action

Empathy &
Altruism

Commitment &
Social Affiliation

Self-Esteem &
Self-Development

Open-Mindedness &
Original Thinking

Self-Awareness &
Artistic Creativity

The Enneagram of the Functions

Patterns and Issues

FLUCTUATING SCORES

If you take the RHETI several times, your basic type should remain the same, although you will probably find that the scores for the other types will rise or fall depending on other influences in your life. Someone having problems with a significant relationship, for instance, is likely to register higher or lower scores in types associated with concerns about relationships, such as Two, Six, and Nine. Someone who has been putting a lot of time and energy into work or is having career problems is likely to produce elevated scores in types Three, Eight, and One. After the troubled relationship or the career issues have been resolved (one way or another), the profile for that person may change yet again. The scores for the person's basic personality type may also be affected, although the type itself should remain the same.

WINGS

In most cases, your (dominant) wing will be indicated by the higher score of one of the types on either side of your basic type. For example, if you test as a Two, your wing will be One or Three, whichever has the higher score.

The second highest *overall* score on the RHETI is not necessarily that of the wing. For instance, a Six's second highest score may be Nine; this does not mean that his or her wing is Nine. (Look at the scores for Five and Seven; the higher is the Six's wing.)

In all cases, the proportion of the wing to that of the basic type must be taken into consideration. Some people will have a relatively high wing score in proportion to their basic type. Some will have a moderate, or even a low, proportion of wing to basic type. This consideration is significant for understanding a person's motivations and behavior, particularly if a prediction of his or her performance is being attempted, as in a business setting. Understanding the relative proportion of the wing to the basic type also yields insights into the childhood origins of the person, codependency issues, and potential pathology. (For a fuller explanation of the proportion of wing to basic type, see *PT*, 312–13.)

In some cases, the "wrong" wing will score higher than a person's actual wing (as determined by subjects themselves or by trained Enneagram judges). An anomaly such as this could result when the qualities of the basic type and the wing are in conflict. In the descriptions of the wings in *Personality Types*, I noted that some combinations of the basic type and wing reinforce each other while other combinations are in conflict. For example, many qualities of the Four and the Three are in opposition, whereas the qualities of the Four and the Five reinforce each other; this situation exists for all the types and their associated wings.

You may also get a high score in a wing other than the one you are expecting because of current factors in your life. For example, someone who had been typed both by himself and by three trained Enneagram teachers as a Seven with a Six-wing tested as a Seven with an Eight-wing. In this instance, although the RHETI correctly diagnosed the subject's basic type, the wing differed from what was expected. A reasonable interpretation is that the subject is in a high-pressure, competitive field where self-confidence and initiative are crucial for success. The subject has been taking more control of his career and has been making a conscious effort to be more assertive. This, coupled with the fact that types Seven and Six are in conflict, possibly caused the subject to register more responses for the Eight than for the Six.

When assessing your wing, it is always a good idea to evaluate the test results by reading the descriptions of both wings in *Personality Types* and deciding which fits you best.

CLOSE CALLS

Occasionally, someone's results will be an almost even distribution of scores among the nine types. Of course, the highest score will usually indicate the basic personality type. However, in some instances, there may be a tie for the high score, and it will therefore be difficult to draw conclusions about the basic type from the evidence of the test alone. Alternatively, while one score may be higher than the others, the scores for several types may be so close that it is difficult to find easily recognizable patterns among them. For example, in a specific case, a subject scored 19 points — his highest score — in three types and 18 points in two others. (This result is discussed at greater length in Case Three in this section.)

There are two explanations for this kind of close pattern. First, the subject may have been engaged in therapy or spiritual development for many years and may have resolved the problems and conflicts of his or her personality. (As we saw in Section 1, as essence is developed, personality loses its grip; hence, the more work a person does on himself or herself, the more it eventually becomes difficult to test personality, and scores would be expected to equalize.) It should be noted, however, that very few individuals seem to have attained this degree of integration and nonidentification with their ego. This explanation should therefore be applied rarely and with great caution.

The second explanation for a relatively close distribution of scores is that the subject may *not* have spent much time in personal development and therefore lacks the self-knowledge necessary to take the RHETI properly. (Ironically, this explanation is the exact reverse of the first.) In this situation, the same pattern results from the subject's identification with too many traits indiscriminately. If this should occur, the subject's personality type may be found by having someone who knows him or her well take the RHETI either with the person or in the person's place (as suggested in Section 4). A subject who has obtained the same score in several types should also carefully read the Profiles in this book and the descriptions in *Personality Types* and *Understanding the Enneagram*, with particular attention to the types' motivations, and then retake the test.

The personality type that most frequently encounters this difficulty is type Nine. Nines have problems seeing themselves because their sense of self is relatively undefined. They have developed their capacity to be unself-conscious and receptive to others and therefore tend to see themselves in all of the types and in none very strongly (although there is a tendency for female Nines to misidentify themselves as Twos, and for male Nines to misidentify themselves as Fives; see *UTE*, 159–61 and 172–76). Furthermore, since Nines also tend to identify strongly with others, they may mistakenly apply the personality traits of loved ones to themselves. For example, Nines married to Fours may register high scores in Four because of their identification with the Four spouse, not necessarily because they have actually developed the qualities of a Four themselves.

Nines are not the only type to misidentify themselves, however. Because of a strongly held self-image, emotional needs, or social fears, individuals of other types may have extreme difficulty seeing themselves accurately and therefore may produce unexpected (even incorrect) test results. A Three, for example, may test almost equally high or higher in another type because he or she invests a great deal in projecting a particular image, especially in his or her career. Threes who want to see themselves as entrepreneurs may test high in Eight, or as intellectuals may test high in Five, or as artists may test high in Four. Furthermore, there is a cultural tendency for females to score high in Two due to socially assigned roles. It is therefore important to read the full description of each type to understand the person's underlying motivations and attitudes to make an accurate assessment.

Beyond this, it is worth noting that some people may not want to admit aspects of themselves either to themselves or to anyone else. Obviously, no test of personality can work unless subjects are willing and able to look at themselves honestly and impartially.

HIGH SCORES TOWARD UNHEALTH

High scores in a subject's Direction of Disintegration do not necessarily mean that the person is unhealthy. Many traits found in the Direction of Disintegration show up in the average range of each type. Furthermore, temporary circumstances in the person's life may elicit high scores in this direction.

The RHETI does not purport to measure health or unhealth, self-actualization or pathology. The primary concern of this test is to discover your basic personality type, and any other conclusions drawn from the test are relatively speculative.

Furthermore, the statements for each type have been designed to fall within the *healthy to average* range of the Levels of Development, that is, between Levels 2 and 6 on the Continuum (see Section 1). It would therefore be virtually impossible for pathology to be discovered by this test. While high scores in the type in your Direction of Disintegration may alert you to troublesome tendencies, the RHETI does not diagnose neuroses or mental disorders.

Remember that if the type in your Direction of Disintegration is understood as a psychological Function, the type is part of your overall personality and, as such, must be integrated into it. All types, no matter how high or low they score on this test, must be taken into consideration.

To further analyze your scores for any type, carefully read the set of 32 statements for the type in Section 7.

Case Studies

The following brief case studies illustrate some of the principles and problems encountered in interpreting the RHETI.

We will first examine a normal pattern of responses that clearly indicated the subject's basic type, wing, and Directions of Integration and Disintegration. The second case is of a subject whose results revealed an unexpectedly elevated score because of conscious efforts he had been making to change his social and economic circumstances. The third case illustrates how relatively flat responses to all nine types can make a diagnosis difficult. The fourth case illustrates a clinical use of the test and the fifth case illustrates fluctuations in the personality functions in the same person tested at different times.

Case One: A Normal Pattern

Type	Two	Three	Four	Five	Six	Seven	Eight	Nine	One
Score									
32									
31									
30					30				
25								26	
20									
		18							
15									
	14		12			14	12		
10									11
				7					
5									
	Two	Three	Four	Five	Six	Seven	Eight	Nine	One

This subject's scores are straightforward and unambiguous: the subject tested as a Six with a Seven-wing; her high score in Nine indicates that she is possibly developing toward her Direction of Integration. The type in her Direction of Disintegration, Three, is also elevated, although this does not necessarily indicate unhealth. In combination with the elevated Nine score, however, it lends further evidence that the subject is a Six. Note that (with the exception of the Five, the intellectual component) most of this subject's other scores were fairly close to the median of 16, indicating a balance of the components of her personality. The relatively low score for Five suggests that the subject may wish to spend more time developing intellectual activities and pursuits. The subject confirmed that she is a Six with a Seven-wing and that the pattern in the chart reflects her experience of herself.

Case Two: An Unexpectedly Elevated Function

Type	Two	Three	Four	Five	Six	Seven	Eight	Nine	One
Score									
32						32			
31									
30									
25									
20		21					20		
			17	17					
15									
10					11			10	10
5	6								
	Two	Three	Four	Five	Six	Seven	Eight	Nine	One

Special circumstances may result in a high score in a type other than a subject's wing, Direction of Integration, or Direction of

Disintegration. In this case, the subject's highest score was in Seven and his second highest score was in Three. By reading the profiles and descriptions in *Personality Types*, the subject confirmed that he is a personality type Seven with an Eight-wing. This was further confirmed by the expert opinion of a trained Enneagram teacher. The subject was puzzled, however, by his high Three score since this was not the type in his Direction of Integration or Disintegration. That outcome was explained by the fact that the subject had been consciously developing himself in a number of personal and professional areas. It was therefore not surprising that Three should emerge as a high score, followed by the type in his Direction of Integration, Five.

In this particular case, not only did the RHETI correctly assess the subject's basic type, wing, and Direction of Integration, the test also indicated the factor that was uppermost in the subject's mind — his personal ambition, as shown by the high score in the type Three Function. Given these findings, the subject felt that the RHETI accurately diagnosed his personality and current concerns.

Case Three: A Close Discrimination
The first time this subject took the test, he scored 19, 19, 18, 19, 11, 17, 18, 9, and 14 in types Two through One, respectively. Because of this unusually flat pattern of responses, the subject was urged to take the test again, and the pattern in the following chart emerged. The subject had been trying to decide whether he was a personality type Four or Five, and the answer became clear, although all of his scores remained close.

As indicated by the scores in the chart, the subject tested as a Four with a Five-wing and confirmed this assessment by reading the descriptions in *Personality Types*. What helped the subject decide whether he was a Four with a heavy Five-wing or a Five with a heavy Four-wing was that in each of the four statements in which he was forced to choose between the Four and the Five, he chose the Four statement.

His flat response patterns in both tests may also have been because the subject is a therapist, has spent years in self-devel-

Case Three: A Close Discrimination

Type	Two	Three	Four	Five	Six	Seven	Eight	Nine	One
Score									
32									
31									
30									
25									
			22						
20	19			19					
		17				16			
15							15		15
					11				
10								10	
5									
	Two	Three	Four	Five	Six	Seven	Eight	Nine	One

opment, and has made conscious efforts at not identifying with his ego or personality. While this explanation is not conclusive, it suggests that some effects of spiritual development may be testable.

Case Four: The Effects of Pathology
As we have previously stated, the RHETI does *not* test how healthy or unhealthy a person is, but if emotional problems are already known to be present, it can suggest areas that may need to be addressed in therapy or counseling. The opinion about this subject by two Enneagram experts was that he is a Nine with an Eight-wing. This finding was confirmed by the RHETI. The outstanding feature of the profile in the chart is the subject's highly elevated score in his Direction of Disintegration, personality type Six. This finding may be due to the subject's alcoholism and feelings of self-destructiveness, low self-esteem, and dependency on his wife and family for his identity. As the chart indicates, his Two score is next highest. While this score is plausible

Case Four: The Effects of Pathology

Type	Two	Three	Four	Five	Six	Seven	Eight	Nine	One
Score									
32									
31									
30									
25					23			24	
20	21		20						
15		15							
						14			
10							11		
									8
5				8					
	Two	Three	Four	Five	Six	Seven	Eight	Nine	One

because he is a parent and breadwinner and has identified with the helper role, the score might also reflect the fact that he feels unappreciated. His high score in Four also indicates problems with self-esteem and depression. Such a pattern, coupled with evidence of alcoholism, would probably be useful to a therapist for better understanding and treating such subjects.

Case Five: Changes in Personality Patterns over Time

The two sets of scores in this chart are for the same subject taken approximately two weeks apart; the first results are in italics, the second set plain. The single number for types Three, Five, and Eight indicate that on both tests the scores were the same.

The subject clearly tested as a Five with a Four-wing in both tests, confirmed by her reading of the descriptions in *Personality Types* and by the opinion of trained Enneagram teachers. It is worth noting that, in both instances, the type in the subject's Direction of Disintegration (Seven) was high, which the subject recognized as her high level of nervous energy as well as restless-

Case Five: Changes in Personality Patterns over Time

Type	Two	Three	Four	Five	Six	Seven	Eight	Nine	One
Score									
32				*32*					
31									
30									
			26						
25									
			22						
20						19			
						16			*16*
15	14	*13*			*14*				14
					12				
10	*10*								
							9	9	
5								8	
	Two	Three	Four	Five	Six	Seven	Eight	Nine	One

ness and uncertainty about her career choices. The score in type Eight, her Direction of Integration, was low, indicating that self-assertiveness and self-confidence, among the Functions of this type, need to be strengthened. Likewise, in both tests, the subject's Nine scores were low, indicating that a lack of receptivity and openness to others is a noteworthy aspect of her personality. This finding is consistent with the fact that the subject twice tested strongly as a personality type Five and, as is characteristic of this type, is highly idiosyncratic and socially detached.

The second significant finding is that, while there were noteworthy variations in some Functions, the subject's basic personality type and the overall "shape" of her profile were similar over time. This finding, replicated by different subjects who have been tested at separate times, indicates that the basic personality type, as predicted, does not change. Various intrapsychic, interpersonal, and environmental factors, however, can cause the other components of the personality to fluctuate somewhat.

7. The Statements Arranged by Type

T HE 144 forced choices in the RHETI contain 288 statements, or 32 statements for each of the nine personality types.

The 32 statements for each type have been grouped here so that you can confirm your test results by seeing them together. The statements begin with those reflecting healthy attitudes and behaviors and move into those expressing average attitudes and behaviors. Note where your responses have clustered. If you agree with most of the statements in the top half of the set, it is unlikely that you are moving toward this type's Direction of Disintegration. Conversely, a majority of responses in the bottom half of the set may be an early warning signal of unhealthy tendencies that you may want to be more aware of. As mentioned earlier, there are no unhealthy (or pathological) attitudes or behaviors reflected in this questionnaire.

PERSONALITY TYPE ONE: *THE REFORMER*

133. Generally, I've been a highly organized, responsible person.
120. I have had a deep need to feel balanced.
138. I usually have followed my conscience and reason.
 79. People have trusted me because I am fair and will do what is right.
111. I've been proud of my ability to take a stand — I've been firm about what I believe in.
 30. I have generally been an earnest, self-disciplined person.
 70. I have thought of myself as a serious, dignified person.
 20. I have tended to be a serious, reserved person who likes discussing issues.

3. I have typically been direct, formal, and idealistic.
51. Generally, I've had strong convictions and a sense of how things should be.
7. I've been more of a "high-minded" idealist.
75. Over the years, my values and lifestyle have remained fairly consistent.
92. I have worried that others' activities would distract me from what I had to do.
66. I've been too serious and strict with myself.
102. Generally, I have not enjoyed losing control of myself very much.
15. It's been difficult for me to take it easy and be more flexible.
61. I've tended to be driven and very hard on myself.
87. I have tended to get into action quickly.
39. Being accepted and well liked has not been a high priority for me.
128. I have generally felt that real love does not depend on physical contact.
142. I have often wondered why people are so happy when so much in life is messed up.
106. I have pushed to get things done correctly, even if it made people uncomfortable.
97. Often, I have helped others see that they are making a mistake.
43. I've tried to motivate people by pointing out the consequences of not following my advice.
56. I have gotten angry when others have not listened to what I have told them.
123. I've tended to see people as disorganized and irresponsible.
25. My habit of telling people what to do has annoyed people.
34. I have been too uncompromising and demanding with others.
12. I have come across as being too sure of myself.
115. I have sometimes put people off by being too uptight.
48. I have not wanted to compromise what is right for friendship.

84. I have often been troubled by anger, perfectionism, and impatience.

PERSONALITY TYPE TWO: *THE HELPER*

71. I've had a caring heart and deep dedication.
35. I've been appreciated for my quiet strength and exceptional generosity.
20. I have tended to be a supportive, giving person who enjoys the company of others.
65. I have provided many people with attention and nurturance.
13. I have been more relationship-oriented than goal-oriented.
29. I have liked to comfort people and calm them down.
 5. I have been a hospitable person and have enjoyed welcoming new friends into my life.
41. People have been interested in me because I've been outgoing, engaging, and interested in them.
116. Being of service and attending to the needs of others has been a high priority for me.
143. I have tried hard not to be seen as a selfish person.
49. I've been a well-meaning supporter.
 8. I have needed to show affection to people.
44. I have often been emotionally demonstrative.
23. I've been too softhearted and sentimental.
95. I have often tried to figure out how I could get closer to others.
53. I have tended to act on my feelings and let the "chips fall where they may."
128. I have given a lot of physical contact to reassure others about how I feel about them.
89. I have had a tendency to come on a little too strong with people.
101. My approach has been to jump in and rescue people.
80. Often, I have been so involved with others that I have neglected my own projects.
92. I have worried that I would be left out of others' activities.

107. I've often taken pride in how important I am in others' lives.

17. My eagerness to have people depend on me has gotten me into trouble with them.

59. I have often been possessive of loved ones — I have had trouble letting them be.

131. I have gotten into trouble with people by being too intrusive and interfering.

85. I realize that I have often been too personal and intimate.

121. In the past, I've probably insisted on too much closeness in my relationships.

113. My own health and well-being have suffered because of my strong desire to help others.

77. I have often felt that my sacrifices have been taken for granted.

56. I have gotten angry when others have not shown enough appreciation for what I have done for them.

125. I've probably been too controlling and manipulative.

137. I have presented myself to others as caring more than I really do.

PERSONALITY TYPE THREE: *THE MOTIVATOR*

57. Being valued and admired has been important to me.

108. I have perceived that I've often come across to others as presentable, even admirable.

81. When meeting someone new, I have usually been poised and self-contained.

111. I've been proud of my ability to be flexible — what's appropriate or important often changes.

117. Typically, I have been even-tempered.

39. I have worked hard to be accepted and well liked.

90. Generally, I have gone out of my way to meet people and make connections.

3. I have typically been diplomatic, charming, and ambitious.

99. When I have disliked people, I have usually tried hard to stay cordial — despite my feelings.

49. I've been a highly motivated go-getter.

13. I have been more goal-oriented than relationship-oriented.
72. I have pursued activities that had a substantial potential for reward and personal recognition.
9. When presented with a new experience, I've usually asked myself if it would be useful to me.
27. I have not depended on people; I have done things on my own.
75. Over the years, my values and lifestyle have changed several times.
63. I have felt uncomfortable making long-term commitments, so I have made major life-changes fairly easily.
18. Usually, I have been able to put my feelings aside to get the job done.
45. I have excelled at dealing with details.
126. I've rarely let self-doubt stand in my way.
67. I've been self-assertive and driven to excel.
31. I've usually liked to let people know what I can do well.
103. I've been overly concerned with doing better than others.
54. Being the center of attention has usually felt natural to me.
36. Much of my success has been due to my talent for making a favorable impression.
129. When I've needed to confront someone, I've often "beaten around the bush" too much.
93. Typically, when I have gotten angry, I have become distant.
85. I realize that I have often been too cool and aloof.
121. In the past, I've probably kept too much distance in my friendships.
135. When I've felt insecure, I've reacted by becoming arrogant and dismissive.
144. I have avoided intimacy when I feared I would not be able to live up to people's expectations of me.
139. Serious adversity has made me feel hardened and resolute.
21. I've often felt the need to perform perfectly.

PERSONALITY TYPE FOUR: *THE ARTIST*

133. Generally, I've been a highly intuitive, individualistic person.

136. I have generally been self-revealing and willing to share my feelings with others.
105. One of my main assets has been my ability to describe internal states.
69. I have spent a lot of time looking inward — understanding my feelings has been important to me.
37. I've prided myself on my originality and inventiveness.
1. I've been romantic and imaginative.
118. Situations that stir up deep, intense emotions have appealed to me.
41. People have been interested in me because I've been quiet, unusual, and deep.
122. I've had a tendency to keep thinking about things from the past.
64. I generally have tended to dwell on my feelings and to hold onto them for a long time.
5. I have been a private person and have not mixed much with others.
90. Generally, I have not gone out of my way to meet people and make connections.
50. When troubled, I have tended to brood about my problems.
18. Usually, I have needed to work through my feelings before I could act.
141. I've had difficulty coping with my feelings and fears, so it's been hard for me to be strong for others.
97. Often, I have not spoken up when I've seen others making a mistake.
73. Fulfilling social obligations has seldom been high on my agenda.
109. I have mostly done what I wanted to do.
46. More often, I have emphasized how different I am from my friends.
25. My habit of being "stand-offish" has annoyed people.
100. Much of my difficulty with people has come from my touchiness and taking everything too personally.
33. When I've had conflicts with others, I've tended to withdraw.

14. I have not been able to speak up for myself very well.
54. Being the center of attention has usually felt strange to me.
82. Generally speaking, I have tended to be pessimistic.
86. I have lost out because I have not felt up to taking opportunities.
10. I have tended to focus too much on myself.
28. I have tended to be moody and self-absorbed.
77. I have often felt too emotionally vulnerable to be around others.
113. My relationships have suffered because of my strong desire to attend to my personal needs.
61. I've tended to be too emotional and rather undisciplined.
126. I've been stopped in my tracks by self-doubt.

PERSONALITY TYPE FIVE: *THE THINKER*

136. I have generally been open-minded and willing to try new approaches.
11. Others have depended on my insight and knowledge.
116. Finding alternative ways of seeing and doing things has been a high priority for me.
68. I've been proud of my clarity and objectivity.
22. I've typically been interested in asking tough questions and maintaining my independence.
72. I have been willing to give up rewards and personal recognition if it meant doing work I was really interested in.
119. I have cared less about practical results than about pursuing my interests.
32. Pursuing my personal interests has been more important to me than having comfort and security.
4. I have tended to be focused and intense.
140. I have usually chosen to depend on as little as possible.
104. My thoughts have generally been speculative — involving my imagination and curiosity.
51. Generally, I've had serious doubts and have questioned how things seemed to be.
15. It's been difficult for me to stop considering alternatives and do something definite.

87. I have tended to take a long time to get into action.
112. My style has leaned toward spareness and austerity.
44. I have seldom been emotionally demonstrative.
64. I generally have tended to minimize my feelings and to not pay very much attention to them.
76. Typically, I have not had much connection with people.
36. Much of my success has been achieved despite my lack of interest in developing interpersonal skills.
8. I have preferred to maintain a certain distance with people.
47. When situations have gotten heated, I have tended to stay on the sidelines.
28. I have tended to be detached and preoccupied.
80. Often, I have been so involved in my own projects that I have become isolated from others.
100. Much of my difficulty with people has come from my not caring about social conventions.
58. When I've debated with friends, I've tended to press my arguments forcefully.
144. I have avoided intimacy when I feared I would be overwhelmed by people's needs and demands.
123. I've tended to see people as intrusive and demanding.
40. In reaction to pressure from others, I have become more withdrawn.
83. I have preferred to inhabit my own little world.
130. I have been attracted to subjects that others would probably find disturbing, even frightening.
108. I have perceived that I've often come across to others as unusual, even odd.
94. I've tended to have trouble falling asleep.

PERSONALITY TYPE SIX: *THE LOYALIST*

120. I have had a deep need to belong.
68. I've been proud of my reliability and commitment.
104. My thoughts have generally been practical — just trying to keep things going.
37. I've prided myself on my perseverance and common sense.
1. I've been pragmatic and down-to-earth.

19. Generally, I've been methodical and cautious.
55. I've been careful, and have tried to prepare for unforeseen problems.
140. I've usually made sure I had some kind of "safety net" to fall back on.
127. I've generally chosen what I knew I already liked: why be disappointed with something I might not like?
32. Having comfort and security has been more important to me than pursuing my personal interests.
73. I have usually taken my social obligations very seriously.
42. Duty and responsibility have been important values for me.
63. I have felt uncomfortable leaving past commitments, so I have had difficulty making major life-changes.
109. I have mostly done what I had to do.
88. I usually have had difficulty making decisions.
91. When I've been unsure of what to do, I've often sought the advice of others.
27. I have depended on my friends and they have known that they can depend on me.
48. I have stood by my friends, even when they have been wrong.
124. Generally, I have not had much confidence in myself.
12. I have come across as being too unsure of myself.
16. I have tended to be hesitant and procrastinating.
114. Generally speaking, I've been too wary and guarded.
23. I've been too hard-nosed and skeptical.
78. I have had a tendency to think of worst-case scenarios.
131. I have gotten into trouble with people by being too evasive and uncommunicative.
52. I've created problems with others by being too pessimistic and complaining.
59. I've often "tested" loved ones to see if they were really there for me.
95. I've often tried to figure out what others want from me.
99. When I have disliked people, I have usually let them know it — one way or another.

6. Generally, it's been easy to "get a rise" out of me.

135. When I've felt insecure, I've reacted by becoming defensive and argumentative.

84. I have often been troubled by nervousness, insecurity, and doubt.

PERSONALITY TYPE SEVEN: *THE GENERALIST*

4. I have tended to be spontaneous and fun-loving.

35. I've been appreciated for my unsinkable spirit and great sense of humor.

71. I've had an agile mind and boundless energy.

60. Coming up with new ideas and getting people excited about them has been one of my major strengths.

30. I have generally been an outgoing, sociable person.

96. I have usually been excitable, fast-talking, and witty.

81. When meeting someone new, I have usually been chatty and entertaining.

19. Generally, I've been adventurous and taken risks.

107. I've often taken pride in my gusto and openness to new experiences.

62. I have tried to keep my life fast-paced, intense, and exciting.

55. I've been spontaneous, and have preferred to improvise as problems come up.

91. When I've been unsure of what to do, I've tried different things to see what worked best for me.

127. Given a choice between something familiar and something new, I have usually chosen something new.

9. When presented with a new experience, I've usually asked myself if it would be enjoyable.

122. I've had a tendency to keep anticipating things I'm going to do.

24. I've often worried that I'm missing out on something better.

76. Typically, I have not had much self-discipline.

132. I've worried that I don't have the self-discipline to focus on what will really fulfill me.

45. Dealing with details has not been one of my strong suits.
50. When troubled, I have tended to find distractions for myself.
86. I have lost out because I have pursued too many possibilities.
134. Being unable to slow down has been one of my main problems.
143. I have tried hard not to be seen as a boring person.
138. I have usually followed my feelings and impulses.
102. Generally, I have enjoyed "letting go" and pushing the limits.
14. I have been outspoken — I've said what others wished they had the nerve to say.
26. Usually, when troubles have gotten to me, I have treated myself to something I've enjoyed.
112. My style has leaned toward excess and overdoing things.
66. I've been too freewheeling and permissive with myself.
98. During most of my life, I have been a stormy person who has had many volatile feelings.
117. Typically, I have had strong changes of mood.
40. In reaction to pressure from others, I have become more aggressive.

PERSONALITY TYPE EIGHT: *THE LEADER*

57. Being independent and self-reliant has been important to me.
105. One of my main assets has been my ability to take charge of situations.
88. I seldom have had difficulty making decisions.
74. In most situations, I have preferred to take the lead.
79. People have trusted me because I am confident and can look out for them.
65. I have provided many people with direction and motivation.
60. Organizing resources and making things happen has been one of my major strengths.
11. Others have depended on my strength and decisiveness.

96. I have usually been measured, straight-talking, and deliberate.

110. I have usually enjoyed high-pressure, even difficult, situations.

119. I have been practical and have expected my work to have concrete results.

101. My approach has been to show people how to help themselves.

29. I have liked to challenge people and "shake them up."

43. I've tried to motivate people by making big plans and big promises.

21. I've often felt the need to be a "pillar of strength."

141. I've had to be strong for others, so I haven't had time to deal with my feelings and fears.

69. I have not spent much time looking inward — getting things done has been important to me.

132. I've worried that I don't have the resources to fulfill the responsibilities I've taken on.

38. Basically, I have been hard-driving and assertive.

24. I've often worried that if I let down my guard, someone will take advantage of me.

47. When situations have gotten heated, I have tended to get right into the middle of things.

83. I have preferred to let the world know I'm here.

93. Typically, when I have gotten angry, I have told people off.

115. I have sometimes put people off by being too aggressive.

33. When I've had conflicts with others, I've rarely backed down.

52. I've created problems with others by being too bossy and controlling.

16. I have tended to be bold and domineering.

2. I have tended to take on confrontations.

129. When I've needed to confront someone, I've often been too harsh and direct.

124. Generally, I have had confidence only in myself.

7. I've been more of a "street-smart" survivor.

137. I have presented myself to others as tougher than I am.

PERSONALITY TYPE NINE: *THE PEACEMAKER*

22. I've typically been interested in maintaining my stability and peace of mind.
98. During most of my life, I have been a steady person in whom "still waters run deep."
38. Basically, I have been easygoing and agreeable.
70. I have thought of myself as a sunny, casual person.
82. Generally speaking, I have tended to be optimistic.
42. Harmony and acceptance have been important values for me.
142. I have often wondered why people focus on the negative when there is so much that's wonderful about life.
46. More often, I have emphasized how much I have in common with my friends.
103. I've been overly concerned with making things OK for others.
89. I have had a tendency to not assert myself enough with people.
98. In most situations, I have preferred to let someone else take the lead.
10. I have tended to focus too much on others.
62. I have tried to keep my life regular, stable, and peaceful.
118. Situations that make me feel calm and at ease have appealed to me.
130. I have preferred not to spend my time dwelling on disturbing, frightening subjects.
78. I have had a tendency to think that everything will work out for the best.
67. I've been modest, and have been happy to go at my own pace.
106. I have not liked feeling pressured, so I have not liked pressuring anyone else.
31. I've usually been shy about showing my abilities.
58. When I've debated with friends, I've tended to let things go to prevent hard feelings.
34. I have given in too easily and let others push me around.

114. Generally speaking, I've been too open and trusting.
110. I have usually disliked being in high-pressure, even difficult, situations.
 17. My reluctance to get too involved has gotten me into trouble with people.
  2. I have tended to avoid confrontations.
134. Overcoming inertia has been one of my main problems.
 94. I've tended to fall asleep easily.
 53. I have tended not to act on my feelings lest they stir up more problems.
 26. Usually, when troubles have gotten to me, I have been able to tune them out.
  6. Generally, it's been difficult to "get a rise" out of me.
125. I've probably been too passive and uninvolved.
139. Serious adversity has made me feel discouraged and resigned.

SECTION 8. Enneagram Interpretations and Contributions

Transmission and Development

The origin of the Enneagram is a mystery and, like all good mysteries, it has kept most of its secrets to itself. Its transmission and development in more recent times, however, are somewhat less mysterious.

The two major figures in the Enneagram's modern development are George Ivanovitch Gurdjieff (c. 1877–1949) and Oscar Ichazo (b. 1931). Both have said that the Enneagram symbol came from sources in distant antiquity and has subsequently appeared in several spiritual traditions. They both believed the Enneagram to be very old, possibly dating to 2500 B.C. or even earlier. (*Ennea-gram* is a Greek word: *ennea* means "nine," and *gram* comes from "graphein," meaning "to write"; hence, the Enneagram is a "nine-figure" or "nine-diagram.")

The first to bring the Enneagram to the West was Gurdjieff, although he never revealed precisely where he discovered it. Since Gurdjieff's death, there have been many speculations about the Enneagram's origins but little or no evidence to support them. While the Enneagram's structure seems to be related to Pythagorean number theory and to Arabic advances in mathematics — and therefore is presumably ancient — there seems to be no reason to doubt that Gurdjieff was introduced to the Enneagram by a Sufi brotherhood, the Naqshbandis, as has been claimed. However, what use the Sufis made of the Enneagram, whether their understanding of the nine personality types was the same as ours, how Gurdjieff was initiated into this secret body of knowledge, what Gurdjieff added to it himself from his extensive travels in search of ancient wisdom, and many other questions, remain unanswered and are probably unanswerable.

We know with certainty that Gurdjieff taught his students about their "Chief Feature" (a manifestation of a person's particular Capital Sin); he sometimes specified which of the various types of "idiots" each of them was. While Gurdjieff's applications clearly indicate that he understood "personality types," it is not clear whether Gurdjieff employed the Enneagram in his teaching of them. Written evidence indicates that he probably did not. If he did, it is peculiar that his students who have written about The Work (as the Gurdjieff system is known) would have omitted this important application of the Enneagram from their many books.

Since this remarkable symbol has, until relatively recently, been transmitted secretly, it is not surprising that it has not been found in written Islamic sources and is extremely rare in other esoteric literature. It would also be surprising if either Gurdjieff or Ichazo had invented the Enneagram himself since neither has claimed to have done so and since the Enneagram has the quality of "something discovered rather than invented" (*PT,* 342). This symbol has a timeless universality about it, and a psychological typology based on it is but one of its many meanings and uses.

ALTHOUGH Gurdjieff was the first westerner to have transmitted the Enneagram from the Middle East, credit for important early work on it goes to the Bolivian mystic and teacher Oscar Ichazo, the founder of the Arica Institute. Ichazo says that he discovered the Enneagram during his travels in Afghanistan in the fifties; he also claims that much of his understanding of the Enneagram resulted from his extensive study of the Kabbalah. Whatever the origins of his insights, Ichazo seems to have been the first to correctly place the nine "passions" (or Capital sins) around the Enneagram symbol. In any case, Ichazo has been secretive about his development and interpretation of the Enneagram and has, to date, revealed his understanding of it only to his own students.

Ichazo began teaching the Enneagram as part of his school for human transformation (Arica) first in Arica, Chile, and later in the United States after founding the Arica Institute in 1970. One of his students, the noted psychiatrist Claudio Naranjo, learned the Enneagram from Ichazo and began teaching it in California shortly after his return from Chile. Since Ichazo has not written in much detail about his interpretation of the Enneagram except in Arica training manuals, it is difficult to evaluate his discoveries fully. It is also difficult to sort out the contributions made solely by Ichazo from those made by Naranjo. What is known is that Naranjo began using his knowledge of other psychological categories to group people by type, and to elicit information from them by interviewing them. This oral interview approach evolved into the method of using panels of exemplars to teach the Enneagram. Naranjo's modern innovation, begun around 1972, has come to be called the "oral tradition," which has been confused with the false notion that there is an ancient oral teaching that has been passed down by Sufis to contemporary Enneagram writers. While it is probable that the Sufis transmitted many other esoteric teachings orally, the Enneagram of personality types as we now know it originated with Ichazo and Naranjo, and has been further explored and developed by subsequent Enneagram authors.

Despite the major seminal discoveries and contributions of Ichazo and Naranjo, the Enneagram remained in a somewhat embryonic state in the early 1970s since the "Arica tradition" (as I have named this interpretation of the Enneagram) was taught confidentially only in Arica schools and therefore was not open to either scholarly or public examination. Furthermore, Ichazo and Naranjo soon broke off relations, and on his return to the United States, Naranjo began teaching his "unauthorized" version of the Enneagram to his own students.

One of them was the Jesuit priest Robert Ochs, who transmitted Naranjo's interpretation to other Jesuit priests and seminarians around North America. They in turn made use of it for spiritual counseling and added their insights to the steadily growing and constantly changing core of oral and written material. The "Jesuit tradition" is thus an offshoot of the "Naranjo tradition"; both are offshoots of the original "Arica tradition" and are somewhat different from it.

When I encountered the Jesuit tradition of the Enneagram in Toronto in 1973 as a Jesuit seminarian, it consisted of nine one-page impressionistic descriptions of the personality types along with several pages of Enneagrams labeled with the names of the ego fixations, the passions, the virtues, the traps, and other material that had been transmitted more or less intact from the Arica tradition. The Jesuit tradition also included oral teachings of its own, some of which made sense, some of which did not. Thus, even in the early seventies, confusion was setting in — and more was to follow — as claims began to be made about what constituted the "authentic teaching."

Unfortunately, confusion and misinformation about the Enneagram have been part of the picture from the beginning of its public dissemination in North America because few had access to the Arica material and those who did were sworn to secrecy. For those working in the Jesuit tradition, the fear of provoking a lawsuit for copyright infringement by using Arica's materials without permission prevented them from publishing their notes and observations about the personality types. A public debate about the relative merits of the various interpretations that were developing seemed hopeless, or at best a distant hope.

A more fundamental reason for confusion was that little of the theory of the Enneagram or of the descriptions of the types had been worked out, at least in the early traditions. Since everything was sketchy and somewhat clandestine, no one knew with any assurance which interpretation was "right," where anything came from, or who had contributed what. Ironically, rather than simply observe human nature to answer questions of interpretation, many in the early traditions began to treat the Enneagram as if it were another dogma to be believed unquestioningly rather than as the living, experiential thing it is.

These problems with the transmission of the Enneagram have taken their toll, and their damage can still be felt today. Confusion about many aspects of the Enneagram's history, development, and transmission is still widespread. How the personality

types themselves are conceived is also confused because, ironically, many generalizations about the types can be made and still
seem plausible. There is enough elasticity and ambiguity in
human nature to disguise a fair amount of lazy thinking and poor
scholarship without being detected easily. Nevertheless, despite
the misinformation flying around in the mid-1970s — and remaining today — the Enneagram has a ring of truth about it. The
seminal discoveries by Ichazo and Naranjo of the nine personality
types revealed a profound understanding of human nature, one
that appealed instantly to a broad spectrum of people.

AS IMPORTANT AS the early work on the Enneagram had
been, I felt that if this system was to have the impact it seemed
to deserve, it would have to be developed in many areas, both in
the descriptions of the nine types and in the understanding of
their underlying structures. One could see that misconceptions
about the types were being taught: some of the types as a whole
were too limited and distorted to account for the vast diversity of
human beings; traits had been mistakenly assigned from one
type to another; important elements were missing, such as a description of the *healthy* side of each type. Even though the early
Enneagram was fascinating, it was also disappointing in its in-
completeness, inconsistencies, and internal contradictions. The
system needed an overhaul.

On September 2, 1975, I began full-time work on the Enneagram, interpreting the Jesuit tradition in the light of Freud, Jung,
Karen Horney, Erich Fromm, and other modern psychologists.
Because I had been introduced to the Enneagram in the Jesuit
tradition, I continued to work in it, although I eliminated the
overtly religious tone and content of that interpretation. I was
and am convinced that the Enneagram is neither primarily religious in nature nor merely another psychological typology, but
an all-encompassing psychology of personality that, among other
things, has profound spiritual implications.

I was greatly aided by my then naive belief that problems with
the Enneagram could be solved quickly and that comprehensive,
self-evidently accurate descriptions of the types could be pro-

duced. That I did not subscribe to any "school" of psychology proved to be a blessing since I was not unduly influenced by a particular point of view — and, more important, I was not discouraged by the prevailing academic opinion that the task I had undertaken was virtually impossible: working out descriptions of universally applicable personality types and discovering their inner mechanics — why they are as they are — is the stuff of age-old fantasies. This was best left to geniuses or madmen. Since I was probably neither and was working alone and could call only on my own observations, intuitions, and reading, the task seemed doomed from the start.

In the end, my ignorance protected me from feeling the full impact of what I had undertaken until I was a few years into my work and realized how vast the task was. But by then I had committed myself to the project and had made several discoveries that allowed me to add fresh material and organize it in a new way. For instance, it is likely that, if I had not discovered the Levels of Development in July 1977, to cite one central innovation, it would have been impossible for me to carry on. But once I had made it, the discovery carried me forward. I am grateful that it did.

IT IS IMPORTANT for everyone interested in the Enneagram to understand that significant differences in interpretation exist among the available Enneagram books. While each has been written from a different point of view and adds certain new insights, numerous contradictions and inaccuracies exist. The results you obtain with the *Riso-Hudson Enneagram Type Indicator* may therefore be different from the assessment you may have made of your personality type based on descriptions found in other books.

For example, you may believe that you are a certain type because you have read other Enneagram books or because you have been "typed" by an Enneagram teacher. The RHETI, however, may indicate that you are another type altogether. To find out which you actually are, please carefully read the full description in *Personality Types*, go to workshops, and talk with experienced Enneagram students to see if the RHETI's assessment actually fits you better than the type with which you have previously identified.

Many of the Enneagram books do not conceive of the personality types in the same way. Some contain misconceptions about the types as a whole (for instance, Eights and Ones, Nines and Fives, Fours and Fives, and Threes and Sevens are often confused). Several books also contain misattributions of traits from type to type, mistaken psychiatric correlations, and misassessments of examples of famous people used to illustrate the types. (For example, Mikhail Gorbachev is listed by some as a type One, Elizabeth Taylor as a type Two, Ronald Reagan as a type Three, and Bette Davis as a type Four. These assessments are far off the mark, and there are many similar mistakes.) Inaccuracies of this kind are understandable, but are unfortunately based on the common tendency to diagnose type on the basis of only one or two traits. Likewise, others have attempted to produce an Enneagram questionnaire for some time but have been unable to do so because, it seems to me, their underlying conception of the types is incomplete or distorted.

Naturally, my own books, including this questionnaire, reflect my evolving understanding of the Enneagram and of human nature. (And like the other books, mine may also contain some mistakes.) Anyone seriously interested in the Enneagram is urged to think critically and to test the validity of the various interpretations for themselves.

A GREAT DEAL of confusion also exists concerning the contributions made by different authors. Misunderstandings about this have been somewhat inevitable since, as noted earlier, the Enneagram was disseminated in the seventies by enthusiasts passing around photocopied notes from the Arica and Jesuit traditions. These notes were usually not attributed to anyone, and so it was extremely difficult to know who had authored them. As books began to be published, some clarity began to emerge, but even so, many assumed that everything about the Enneagram belonged to an ancient "oral tradition" and was therefore in the public domain — or, worse, that everyone was borrowing from everyone else and that no one had done any original work in the field.

This is certainly not the case, and as the Enneagram becomes better known, it is all the more necessary to have a clearer idea of the origins of the various interpretations now in circulation for two reasons: first, there is no ancient authority in any "oral tradition" which can ultimately be referred to as the "correct" and "authentic" teaching. This, of course, implies that there is no historically sanctioned method of teaching the Enneagram. Second, the contemporary books on the Enneagram are the result of the work and research of their respective authors and are not merely variations on a traditional teaching. Therefore, the work of these authors is copyrightable and not in the public domain. Unfortunately, we will have to wait for an independent, critical history of the Enneagram to be written for all of the claims and counterclaims to be adequately sorted out. Until someone undertakes to produce such a book, Enneagram writers have an obligation to inform their readers about which tradition they are working in, where they have obtained their source material, how they have developed it, and what original contributions they themselves have made.

In an attempt to fulfill these obligations, I previously stated that "everything in *Personality Types* and in [*Understanding the Enneagram*] that has not been explicitly attributed to someone else or to a specific traditional source is the result of my original work" (*UTE*, 17). I then made a few comments about how I discovered the Levels of Development and the childhood origins of the types and produced my own type names and so forth, without, however, providing a complete list of my discoveries "for the record." I believed that this general statement would be enough to clarify what I had contributed to the development of the Enneagram.

I was wrong. My publisher, Houghton Mifflin, and I are therefore taking the opportunity provided by the publication of this book to set forth my discoveries. Almost all of them have, to date, been published either in *Personality Types* or in *Under-*

standing the Enneagram. With the exception of the "Psychic Structures" (number 10 in the following list), most of them have either been mentioned or implied in these two books. However, not all of them were taught explicitly except in our Professional Training Programs. *Personality Types* contains a great deal of information "in between the lines" — for instance, the defense mechanisms, the Basic Fears, and the Basic Desires for the types are given in each description, although without being specified directly. (In *Understanding the Enneagram,* I was explicit about more material and will be even more explicit in future books.)

With apologies for the immodesty of the following list — but with the hope that readers will understand its necessity — the following are among my contributions to Enneagram theory and practice.

1. The complete *systematic description* of each of the nine personality types. Clarifying and elaborating the impressionistic sketches from the Jesuit tradition to detailed descriptions of approximately 10,000 words for each type found in *Personality Types.*

2. The nine *Levels of Development* within each personality type and how they are structured into healthy, average, and unhealthy areas of functioning; the internal symmetries between the Levels, and the 81 descriptive titles given to each Level ("The Inspired Creator" and "The Self-Aware Intuitive" for personality type Four, and so forth, for all the types).

3. The developmental *Childhood Origins* for each type and how they are responsible for each type's basic motivations, sense of self, cognitive style, and overall pattern of traits. (More about this will be published in the forthcoming *Working with the Enneagram.*)

4. The *Basic Fear* and *Basic Desire* for each type and how the effects of these primary motivations continue to be felt in the subsequent *secondary motivations* (fears and desires) at each Level of Development for each type.

5. The most comprehensive published explanations for and descriptions of the *Direction of Integration* and *Direction of Disintegration* for each type, thus revealing a dynamic, predictive quality to the Enneagram.

6. The elucidation of the *full range of traits for each type*, adding hundreds of observations per type to the existing sketches in the Jesuit material. Of special note, the discovery and development of the *healthy* traits for each type, thus overcoming one of the main criticisms of the Arica and Jesuit interpretations, namely, that they were too negative.

7. The *structural interrelationships* between the personality types (such as "reversals," "acting out," the "Functions," and other internal connections, most of which will be published in *Working with the Enneagram*). Demonstrating the internal coherence of the personality types indicates the subtlety, sophistication, and complexity of the Enneagram as a multidimensional system.

8. The introduction of numerous innovations in the *terminology* used to describe the types ("Directions of Integration and Disintegration," the "Relating Triad," "basic type," "primary" and "secondary" types, "characteristic temptation," and "saving grace," among other new terms). Similarly, producing appropriate, *positive descriptive labels* for the types as a whole: "The Reformer" for the One, "The Helper" for the Two, "The Motivator" for the Three, and so forth.

9. The descriptions of and rationale for the *wing* of each type, including the irregular relationship of the wing(s) to the basic type (that is, that some are in conflict with the basic type, while others reinforce the basic type). Also, the *dynamics of the wings* — how they integrate and evolve, as does the basic personality type.

10. The *Psychic Structures* for each type. The Psychic Structures (to be published in *Working with the Enneagram*) are pictorial models indicating the psychological activities that occur at each Level of Development for each type.

11. The *defense mechanisms* associated with each personality type. There are at least three distinct yet interrelated defense mechanisms for each type, as listed in *Understanding the Enneagram*, 44–85.

12. How the personality types of the Enneagram (properly delineated) correspond with the *psychiatric personality disorders* as well as other classification systems (Freud, Jung, Horney, Fromm, the *DSM*-III(R); for example, correspondence of Horney's aggressive, compliant, and withdrawn types to types Three, Seven, and Eight; One, Two, and Six; and Four, Five, and Nine, respectively.

13. Numerous *new features* and teaching aids, including the short profiles found in *PT* and *UTE* as well as in this book; the recommendations for personal growth, the abstract structural patterns of each type; and practical business applications of the Enneagram (that will be available to my students as *The Enneagram Management Manual*).

Despite these discoveries, my understanding of human nature is still only beginning to unfold. This is, indeed, a life's work worth doing. I not only have much to learn but also much for which to give thanks, especially for the opportunity to take part in bringing the wonderful gift of the Enneagram to the world.

SECTION 9. A Note on Validation

THE *Riso-Hudson Enneagram Type Indicator* is subject to ongoing research and field testing and will be revised in subsequent printings as necessary. Preliminary validation studies prior to publication indicate that the RHETI is 85 to 90 percent accurate for identifying a person's basic personality type. This finding has been determined by correlating the questionnaire results with the subjects' assessments of their types as well as with the assessments of one or more expert Enneagram judges.

Qualified individuals who wish to conduct validation studies on the *Riso-Hudson Enneagram Type Indicator* are invited to contact the authors at Enneagram Personality Types, Inc., 222 Riverside Drive, Suite 10, New York, New York 10025.

Your local bookstore can provide you with copies of all of Don Richard Riso's books: *Personality Types* (1987), *Understanding the Enneagram* (1990), *Discovering Your Personality Type: The New Enneagram Questionnaire* (1995), and *Enneagram Transformations* (1993). Or you can order them from the publisher by calling (800) 225-3362.

To obtain multiple copies for use in Enneagram Workshops, as well as business and organizational settings, please contact Houghton Mifflin Company, Special Sales Department, 215 Park Avenue South, New York, New York 10003, or phone (212) 420-5890. Special discounts are available for orders of ten copies or more.

To contact Don Richard Riso and Russ Hudson for information about their Enneagram Workshops, professional trainings, new publications, and business seminars, or to have your name added to your mailing list for Workshops in your area, please contact Enneagram Personality Types, Inc., at the address below.

For personal consulting or to have the *Riso-Hudson Enneagram Type Indicator* interpreted by an Enneagram teacher trained and certified by Don Richard Riso and Russ Hudson, please contact Enneagram Personality Types, Inc., for a referral to a teacher in your area.

To order a self-scoring offprint of the *Riso-Hudson Enneagram Type Indicator*, please call the phone number listed below.

Enneagram Personality Types, Inc.
222 Riverside Drive, Suite 10
New York, N.Y. 10025
212-932-3306
212-865-0962 (fax)

Enneagram Resources by Don Richard Riso

DISCOVERING YOUR PERSONALITY TYPE
The New Enneagram Questionnaire (1992, 1995)

The best general introduction to using the Enneagram, this book contains a highly accurate personality test that identifies basic personality types to yield a complete psychological profile.
Houghton Mifflin, ISBN 0-618-21903-X

ENNEAGRAM TRANSFORMATIONS
Releases and Affirmations for Healing Your Personality Type (1993)

In this groundbreaking work, Riso offers readers the opportunity to take a psychological inventory of inner strengths that can be invaluable for self-development and all forms of recovery.
Houghton Mifflin, ISBN 0-0395-65786-5

PERSONALITY TYPES
Using the Enneagram for Self-Discovery (1987, 1996)

Revised with Russ Hudson. This new edition updates the descriptions of the nine personality types and greatly expands the accompanying guidelines, uncovering the Core Dynamics, or Levels of Development, within each type.   Houghton Mifflin, ISBN 0-395-79867-1

UNDERSTANDING THE ENNEAGRAM
The Practical Guide to Personality Types (1990, 2000)

With Russ Hudson. This authoritative guide to the Enneagram is an indispensable resource that teaches not only how to understand this psychological framework in daily life but how to use it in many different settings.   Houghton Mifflin, ISBN 0-618-00415-7

THE WISDOM OF THE ENNEAGRAM
The Complete Guide to Psychological and Spiritual Growth for the Nine Personality Types (1999)

With Russ Hudson. This guide to the psychology and spirituality of the Enneagram system offers a clear map of the nine paths to our highest self-expression.   Bantam Doubleday Dell, ISBN 0-553-37820-1